Cadet Nurse
S T O R I E S
THE CALL FOR AND RESPONSE OF WOMEN DURING WORLD WAR II

THELMA M. ROBINSON · PAULIE M. PERRY

Center Nursing Publishing

Publishing Director: Jeff Burnham
Book Acquisitions Editor: Fay L. Bower, RN, DNSc, FAAN
Graphic Designer: Bruce L. Williams
Communication Manager: Frank Maez
Copy Editor: Estelle Beaumont, RN, PhD
Proofreader: Linda Canter

Thanks go to Women in Military Service for America Memorial Foundation, Inc., for their support and assistance in the production of this book.

Printed in the United States of America
Composition by Center Nursing Publishing
Printing/binding by Printing Partners
Cover, "The Girl With A Future" (Second year poster)
    by U.S. Department of Health and Human Services
    Photo courtesy of National Archives and Records
    Administration

Honor Society of Nursing, Sigma Theta Tau International
Center Nursing Publishing
550 West North Street
Indianapolis, IN 46202
www.nursingsociety.org

ISBN: 1-930538-03-0

02 03 04 05 / 9 8 7 6 5 4

Dedicated to Lucile Petry Leone,
Emeritus Chief Nurse and
Director of the Cadet Nurse Corps,
United States Public Health Service,
Department of Health and Human Services;

and to

the women who shared their cadet nurse stories.

Lucile Petry, Director, Cadet Nurse Corps

Surgeon General Parran appointed Lucile Petry
(Leone) director of the newly established Division
of Nurse Education. She became the first woman
to head a major U.S. Public Health Service
division.

Contents

Acknowledgments

This book is the culmination of an 8-year project of searching for and reviewing archival materials and collecting stories from cadet nurses of World War II. In an effort to weave historical data with the most representative and vivid stories, we are forever grateful to the many who have helped us with the task of recording cadet nurse experiences.

We owe special thanks to the archivists and librarians who helped us at the National Archives and Records Administration in Washington, D.C., the Library of Medicine in Bethesda, Maryland, university libraries in Denver and Aurora, Colorado, and Anchorage and Eagle River of Alaska.

We appreciate those who helped in our search for former cadet nurses and others associated with the Cadet Nurse Corps as we recruited storytellers. We also extend thanks to:

- the United States Public Health Service who supported our poster session at the Cadet Nurse Corps Commemorative Conference, May 1994, in Bethesda, Maryland;
- Claire Martin, former dean of the University of Colorado School of Nursing, who encouraged our early beginnings;
- the schools of nursing alumni associations who provided names of former cadets; and
- the many people who talked about our project to fellow cadet nurses and friends.

We are fortunate to have had help publicizing our project, and we thank the *American Nurse*, in which Thelma's letter seeking cadet nurses was published, and Kaylene Johnson for her article, "Call of the Nightingales-Nurse Cadet Sisters

Summon Memories of the Corps," which appeared in *Senior Voice* of Alaska.

We are indebted to those who critiqued our manuscript and helped us improve our writing style: the Anchorage Writer's Guild; the nonfiction writing class at the University of Alaska; Dr. Susan Johnson, author and critic, as well as other cadets and friends. Dr. John Parascandola, United States Public Health Service historian, provided immeasurable assistance for retrieving archival photos and information regarding the United States Cadet Nurse Corps. Dr. Parascandola also spent many hours reviewing and giving suggestions and perspectives on the entire manuscript. To Dr. Fay L. Bower we extend our heartfelt thanks for her confidence and expertise in finalizing our manuscript. Working with Dr. Bower and Paul Branks, director of Center Nursing Press, was an exhilarating finish to our long endeavor.

To our children, Susi, Bill, and Mary Lee; Dennis, Mary Louise, Larry, and Bruce we declare our deepest appreciation for continued encouragement and confidence in the writing and publishing of this book.

Paulie gives special recognition to her son-in-law, Mark, for his assistance in designing our brochure, his computer expertise, and his understanding and support to the end of his days.

To Dick, Thelma's husband and best friend for more than 50 years, who cheered us on every step of the way, Thelma gives her deepest gratitude.

Last, and most important, we thank the cadet nurses themselves as well as the consultants, directors of nursing, instructors, and our esteemed Emeritus Chief Nurse of the U.S. Cadet Nurse Corps, Lucile Petry Leone. These people shared their experiences so that the story of the Corps could be told from a personal point of view.

Their support, enthusiasm, and appreciation for our project inspired us to forge ahead toward our goal, and we shall not forget their valuable contributions.

Paulie M. Perry, AD, RN, PHN (Retired)
Thelma M. Robinson, RN, MSN, PNP

Preface

John Parascandola, PhD
Public Health Service Historian

The Cadet Nurse Corps was a massive and important federal program for the training of American nurses during the Second World War. In the few years (1943-48) of the program's existence, it graduated some 124,000 nurses at a time when nursing services were especially crucial to the nation. Most of the cadets went on to have productive careers in the nursing profession, making valuable contributions to health care in the United States. The administration of the program was vested in the Public Health Service, under the brilliant leadership of Lucile Petry. The story of this short-lived but highly significant program deserves to be told in detail, and this fine book by Thelma Robinson and Paulie Perry fills that need by providing a comprehensive and very readable account of the U.S. Cadet Nurse Corps. In addition to chronicling the history of the corps and assessing its contributions, the authors also allow us to share the experiences of many of the cadets themselves in their own words. Robinson and Perry systematically collected the reminiscences of more than 380 former Cadets as part of their research for the book. This work is a substantial contribution to the history of nursing and of federal support of health professions training.

Rockville, MD
October 26, 2000

Introduction

The U.S. Cadet Nurse Corps comprised the largest and youngest group of uniformed women to serve their country during World War II and the early postwar years (1943-1948). Cadet nurses, under the auspices of the United States Public Health Service (USPHS), served while they learned. Reporting to the House Committee on Military Affairs on February 6, 1945, Surgeon General Thomas Parran of the USPHS said:

> The Cadet Nurse Corps is accomplishing important results in civilian nursing, not merely by providing badly needed nursing care but also by replacing and releasing graduate nurses (for the war). It is estimated that students in nursing schools are giving 80% of nursing care in their affiliated hospitals. The recruitment program of the United States Cadet Nurse Corps has contributed immeasurably toward preventing a collapse of nursing care in civilian hospitals ("Cadet Nurse Corps," 1945, p. 995).

The U.S. Cadet Nurse Corps law was in effect as of July 1, 1943, and gave women as young as 17 years old the opportunity to serve their country in uniform as nurses. Recruiting slogans, "A Lifetime Education-Free" and "The Girl with a Future, Be a Cadet Nurse" appealed to high school graduates. Between July 1, 1943 and October 15, 1945, 179,000 young women joined the Corps and 124,065 graduated from 1,125 participating schools of nursing (U.S. Federal Security Agency, 1950).

To become cadet nurses, young people-mostly young women-first enrolled in state-approved schools of nursing participating in the Corps program. When they joined the Corps, tuition, books, a stipend, and a uniform were provided. In return they promised to serve as nurses for the duration of the war, which included serving in a civilian or military hospital, the Indian Health Service, or other public health facilities.

We are sisters, and Thelma was 16 and Paulie 14 when the Japanese bombed Pearl Harbor, forcing our country out of isolationism into global war. Like other citizens, we asked ourselves, "What can I do to help win the war?" Two and 4 years later, respectively, a significant opportunity was available for us. We joined the U.S. Cadet Nurse Corps. Even though we served at different times, we experienced the full Corps program, beginning with the first year of recruitment in 1943 and ending with the last class graduating in 1948 (after the war). Although historians of nursing record the importance of the Corps, little has been written about the personal experiences of the women who served in the Corps. We originally planned to write about just our own cadet nurse experiences, but we soon realized our stories were hardly representative of the thousands of untold cadet nurse experiences.

We wanted to learn the answers to the following questions: Who were the people who chose to serve their country during World War II as cadet nurses? Where did they come from? Would they have become nurses without the U.S. Cadet Nurse Corps? What do they most vividly remember about their experiences as cadet nurses? Having been offered a lifetime education free, what do former cadet nurses say about that promise?

After searching for and reading original Corps documents in the National Archives and libraries, our enthusiasm soared. We invited former cadet nurses throughout the country to help us tell the cadet nurse story from both a historical and personal point of view.

We distributed our brochure, "The Cadet Nurse Corps-A Story Unfolding" to more than 2,000 cadet nurse alumnae

(Robinson & Perry, 1993). More than 380 women, representing 121 schools of nursing in 33 states plus the District of Columbia, responded over 5 years. Helen Siehndel Meyer's reply was typical. She said, "Recently, we held a World War II commemorative program. Not a single person viewing our exhibits knew about the Cadet Nurse Corps."

The women who wrote to us wanted to know how they could take part in our project. We designed and distributed a response guideline to help people tell how they learned about the U.S. Cadet Nurse Corps and to describe what they saw and heard during their days as cadet nurses. Former cadet nurses began browsing through scrapbooks, photo albums, and other memorabilia. They read diaries and old letters to jog their memories. From Washington, D.C., to San Francisco, from Minot, North Dakota, to Waco, Texas, many women met in small groups and reminisced about their years in the Corps.

Many former cadets expressed interest and support but sent regrets that they could not participate because of health problems or other reasons. We are a vulnerable group, now ranging in age from 72 to 96. But more than 380 former cadet nurses and other women associated with the Corps did share their stories through interviews and written responses. Many women sent memorabilia as well.

We also visited with former U.S. Cadet Nurse Corp Director Lucile Petry Leone (now deceased), who graciously shared materials, photos, and memories.

We learned that other cadet nurses came from families hard hit by the Great Depression, just as we did. Many of our families could not have afforded a college education for us. Together we are the women who seized the opportunity to meet the challenge to become cadet nurses.

As cadet nurses we recall a time of camaraderie with our colleagues when we lived together in nurses' residences. We remember a time when many of the boys went off to war and it was all right for young women to dance together; a time when we launched ships and marched in parades; when we cared for military personnel who were injured in battle and then returned to their homeland. We worked side by side with Sister Kenny, the polio messiah from Australia. It was a time when nurses changed the course of treatment for polio from splints and casts to hot packs and muscle retraining. With new information and skills, nurses encouraged polio victims to walk again. It was a time when penicillin, more precious than gold, was given in a suspension of beeswax. And it was a time when we, the cadet nurses, gave those first life-saving penicillin shots.

Most of the cadet nurse students trained in hospital schools of nursing based on monastic, military, and medical traditions. But 10% share memories of a progressive nurse education, obtained at college and university schools of nursing and a few atypical hospital schools of nursing. These latter schools established a precedent in the advancement of nurse education and the design of a new role for nurses in the future. The challenge to tradition is an important part of this story.

Why do so few remember us? Why did we, cadet nurses of World War II, not consider ourselves significant in a historical sense? Perhaps the selflessness of our nurse training was so inbred that we made little effort to draw attention to our record. Perhaps we simply did not take the time to tell our stories. Now 50 plus years later, we must tell our families and friends about the part we played in winning World War II on the home front. We have an advantage in telling the cadet nurse story. We were in the Corps.

References

The cadet nurse corps. (1945). JAMA, 127(4), 995.

Perry, P.M., & Robinson, T.M. (1994). Cadet nurse corps: A story unfolding. [Brochure]. Aurora, CO: Authors.

U.S. Federal Security Agency. (1950). The U.S. cadet nurse corps 1943-1948. (PHS Publication No. 38, p. 97). U.S. Government Printing Office.

1

AVERTING A CRISIS
by Thelma M. Robinson

On January 6, 1941, our family, like many others, huddled around a battery-powered radio prepared to listen to President Franklin Delano Roosevelt's 15th Fireside Chat. The Battle of Britain raged as dictators throughout the world conquered one country after another. Renowned editors and others debated our country's stand. How long could we remain uninvolved in this war-torn world?

Our president had just been elected to his third term (an unprecedented event) and on this night promised to answer questions Americans had been asking. He began his talk with "My friends and fellow Americans" as if we were gathered around his fireplace. I listened carefully to our president's words because the next day my high school classmates and I would be discussing the president's speech in our American History class. Mr. Roosevelt said:

> How great is the danger? Never before has our American civilization been in such danger. Why is this war a concern of the United States? If Great Britain goes down, all of us in the Americas will be living at the point of a gun. The vast resources and wealth of this hemisphere constitute the most tempting loot in the world. What's to be done? Arms, more and faster ... more planes, tanks, guns, freighters. Required soon might be rationing of consumer and luxury goods. We must be the great arsenal of democracy (Dille, 1968, pp. 9-10).

Dad turned off the radio, leaned back in his rocking chair and said, "Thank God, we're staying out of the war." The drought of the '30s had ended; crops once more were bountiful. Neighbors and relatives were moving west to work in the war industries. Life was good.

On December 7, 1941, our family went to church as usual. There we learned that the Japanese had bombed Pearl Harbor, wherever that was. At high school the next day, my classmates and I filed into the assembly area to listen to the radio broadcast of President Roosevelt's brief, emotional speech to Congress. Now, virtually the entire world was at war. Two days later our president said:

> On the road ahead there lies hard work ... grueling work ... day and night, every hour and every minute. I was about to add that ahead there lies sacrifice for all of us. But it is incorrect to use that word. The United States does not consider it a sacrifice to do all one can, to give one's best to our nation, when the nation is fighting for existence and its future life ("President Roosevelt," 1942, p. 16).

Little did I understand the state of our country's health at that time. Years later I visited libraries and archives and learned about the health conditions of our country during World War II. I discovered that great cities of industrial workers sprang up overnight as many small towns doubled in population causing inadequate sewer systems, an increase in rodents, and the threat of disease. Sanitation of public eating-places broke down, and when no one was available to provide needed immunizations, clinics were cancelled. In some instances even hospitalization was not available. Many births took place at home without midwives, and physicians were very overworked. Dr. William Shepard, a West Coast public health physician, said he was afraid the war would be lost on the home front ("When Does the Home Front," 1943).

The demand for civilian and military nurses escalated. The United States Public Health Service (USPHS) appointed additional public health nurses to supplement local staffs but could not keep up with the demand. And each month the American Red Cross Nursing Service recruited hundreds of nurses for the Army. Dozens of nurses also volunteered for service with the Navy and Naval Reserve (Amidon, 1941).

Civilian hospitals throughout the country were filled to capacity when the defense boom began. Financial prosperity of farmers, wage earners, and white-collar workers, as well as 3-cents/day hospitalization insurance plans, brought more patients to hospitals and clinics for operations and treatments. Each year the birth rate increased and hospital care was needed for the wives and children of servicemen. The war progressed and the nurse shortage worsened ("Wartime Nursing," 1943).

I learned about the people and events that shaped the Cadet Nurse Corps. One influential nurse leader was Isabel Maitland Stewart, who wrote about the way nursing education was in conflict with the very concepts of nursing. She noted that young women who chose nursing for a career possessed a strong desire for service and a concern for human need. However, excessive discipline during the educational process frequently became obtrusive; too often the education was authoritarian and oppressive. Stewart advocated resolving these inconsistencies within the profession by placing nurse education on a more democratic basis.

> By helping to defend democracy we may help bring about our own professional emancipation, achieve our full professional maturity, and win for our educational system [of nursing] the measure of support it has a right to ask from the society which we serve (Stewart, 1940, p. 1382).

Could nursing meet the challenge to increase services and at the same time improve the quality of nursing education on a national scale during wartime? There was no question that nurses were essential in national defense, social welfare, and safety. However, Isabel Stewart, who grew up in a family where daughters had the same educational opportunities as sons, observed that Uncle Sam had no money for nurses. The government provided funds for the training of men as military officers, physicians, airplane pilots, mechanics, industrial workers, and engineers. Stewart said nurses stood ready to care for men ... to go into the front-line trenches wherever the battle raged against disease.

Nurse leaders, determined to pursue new objectives in the spirit of democracy, took an active step forward. The Nursing Council on National Defense, with representatives from five national nursing organizations, the Red Cross, and six federal agencies, inventoried the nursing forces (Nursing Council on National Defense, 1940). The Council found the number of nurses insufficient to meet the demands for nursing services throughout the country ("The National Survey," 1941).

As physicians left for military service, nurses took over more of the health care. In response to the need for nurses, the American Red Cross trained thousands of volunteers to take over some of the duties of nurses in hospitals. Hospitals closed some wards to lighten the civilian demand for nursing (U.S. Federal Security Agency, 1950).

One plan to ease the shortage was to recruit more young women into nursing schools. As Isabel Stewart pointed out, most of the students' education was in the hospital providing care so they were an obvious source of nursing service that was badly needed in civilian and military hospitals. In fact, during this time, students provided the largest percentage of nursing service in hospitals that were affiliated with nursing schools. Thus an increase in the number of students could compensate for the loss of registered nurses to military service (Stewart, 1941).

Nurse leaders and other advocates realized schools of nursing would need support if this plan was adopted. So in 1941 Congress appropriated $1,200,000 for nursing, and then almost doubled the appropriation in 1942. The funds provided refresher courses for inactive graduate nurses and support for the increased enrollment in basic schools of nursing. With the mushrooming demand from civilian and military populations, however, the appropriated federal monies were not enough to meet the national nurse shortage (U.S. Federal Security Agency, 1950).

On March 29, 1943, Mrs. Frances P. Bolton, congresswoman from Ohio, friend to nurses, and one of the wealthiest women in the country, introduced H.R. 2326. This bill would provide for the training of nurses for the armed forces, governmental and civilian hospitals, health agencies, and war industries through grants to the institutions providing the training. The Senate companion bill, introduced by Senator Josiah W. Bailey of North Carolina, added an amendment that barred discrimination against race, creed, or color (U.S. Federal Security Agency, 1950).

Marion W. Sheahan from the National Nursing Council for War Service (formerly the Council for Defense), which represented both private and governmental agencies, summarized the need for a nurses' training program by saying:

> We in the profession feel we have done all we can ... in order to compete with all of the other attractions for young women, through industry paying large salaries, through other women's activities of the government ... the WAC, the WAVES, and SPARS ... there must be some evidence that the government considers ... nursing essential (U.S. Federal Security Agency, 1950, p. 16).

During the hearings the strongest case for the nurse-training program came from hospital authorities who repeatedly testified that nursing care in civilian hospitals was in a desperate state. Letters and telegrams in support of the bill poured into government offices ("Program for Recruiting," 1943).

Legislation creating the Nursing Training Act passed both houses unanimously. On June 15, 1943, the Bolton Act, as it was commonly called, was ready for the signature of the president. As provided by law, an advisory committee of nursing and related professional groups was appointed by the U.S. Federal Security Administration to draft rules and regulations for the newly established nurse corps (U.S. Federal Security Agency, 1950).

The Advisory Committee met on June 25, 1943. Two names for the nurse corps were proposed: Victory Nurse Corps and Student War Nursing Reserve. Committee member Marion G. Howell, director of the Frances Payne Bolton School of Nursing at Western Reserve University in Ohio, made the motion to adopt the name of *United States Cadet Nurse Corps*. Dr. Oliver C. Carmichael, president of Vanderbilt University in Nashville, Tennessee, seconded the motion and the committee's vote was unanimous (U.S. Federal Security Agency, 1950). The rules and regulations were finalized and the Nurse Training Act became Public Law No. 74 on July 1, 1943 (Nurse Training Program, 1943).

President Roosevelt signs Nurse Training Act. On June 15, 1943, President Roosevelt signed into law the bill that created the Nurse Training Act, which later became known as the Bolton Act. Surgeon General Thomas Parran looked on.

The USPHS established the Division of Nurse Education, to be directly responsible to the Surgeon General. The new division was to administer the Bolton Act appropriation, which amounted to more than 50% of the entire USPHS budget. Surgeon General Thomas Parran appointed Lucile Petry (a nurse) to serve as director of the U.S. Cadet Nurse Corps. She became the first woman to head a USPHS division.

On July 5, 1943, the rules and regulations were approved by Surgeon General Parran and published in the Federal Register on July 9, 1943. In issuing the regulations the surgeon general emphasized that no one federal pattern would be set. He said:

> The schools (of nursing) are free to select students, to plan curricula, and to formulate policies consistent with the Act and the traditions of the institutions concerned. This is a partnership job between the USPHS, the institutions, and the students. I am confident that through continued teamwork we shall achieve the goal, which means so much to the health of our country (Parran, 1943, p. 29-30).

Student nurses who joined the Corps promised to remain active in nursing in either military or essential civilian nursing services for the duration of the war. The promise did not bar marriage. The surgeon general explained that students would be available for full-time nursing at an earlier date and would guarantee a continuous supply of graduate nurses for the duration of the war.

The surgeon general urged schools of nursing to move quickly providing mechanisms for recruitment and selection. All state-accredited schools of nursing were eligible if they agreed to accelerate their programs and arrange for each senior cadet to complete a 6-month residency in her home hospital, a state or federal hospital, or other public health service facility. The U.S. Cadet Nurse Corps called for an enrollment of 65,000 student nurses in basic schools of nursing during the first fiscal year (1943-1944). Postgraduate scholarships for special training in obstetric, pediatric, and psychiatric nursing would also be available.

Many years later I had the pleasure to meet and talk with former Assistant Surgeon General Lucile Petry Leone, USPHS. More than 50 years previous to our meeting, I had promised to serve my country as a nurse until the end of World War II. Corps Director Petry's signature verified my certificate of membership in the U.S. Cadet Nurse Corps. I tingled with excitement as I waited to meet her. This grand lady's leadership of the Corps opened horizons in nursing as a profession, in nursing education, and in service. Her rise to assistant surgeon general created career pathways in the uniformed services for women and nurses who followed. Below is a conversation she and I had (L. P. Leone, personal communication, March 24, 1994).

The existence and success of the U.S. Cadet Nurse Corps was because of three outstanding leaders. Representative Frances Payne Bolton (left) introduced legislation on March 29, 1943, that established the U.S. Cadet Nurse Corps. Surgeon General Thomas Parran (center) administered the U.S. Cadet Nurse Corps program. Director Lucile Petry (right) successfully instituted the many facets of the program and was its only director.

Q. Nurse leaders and others had different opinions on how to resolve the nurse shortage during World War II. How was consensus reached in such record time?

A. Much credit is due Mrs. Elmira Bears Wickenden, the executive director for the National War Council. She was adept and skilled in working with people, always listening, always guiding. Her remarkable ways brought people together in decision making. In 1947 President Truman recognized Mrs. Wickenden's wartime service by awarding her the Medal of Merit for her work with the Cadet Nurse Corps.

We had to agree; we had to move ahead. We had to win … we had to win the war!

Fifty years earlier, not many miles away in the shipyards of Richmond, California, Cadet Nurse Rachel Dole swung the champagne bottle that launched the S.S. Duke of Victory off to war. Dole, a student at Stanford University School of Nursing, was cadet nurse number 140,000 to join the Corps ("Cadet Nurse," 1945).

Q. Compared to today's implementation of federal laws, the time frame from conception to delivery of the Cadet Nurse Corps was incredibly fast. How did that happen?

A. As soon as the Cadet Nurse Corps was created, Surgeon General Thomas Parran sent a detailed telegram to every school of nursing describing the program and inviting its participation. I joined Surgeon General Parran and Eugenia Spalding, assistant director, in barnstorming for 2 weeks in 22 cities across the country. Large meetings were held for representatives from schools of nursing, hospitals, and universities who came with questions about the newly formed Cadet Nurse Corps. The nurse corps was a way to prevent the collapse of our hospitals and to meet the nursing needs of the armed services while allowing nursing students to complete their education and serve their country at the same time.

I'll never forget our first meeting. There had been no time for Tom and me to plan what we would do. Tom looked trim and handsome in his military uniform with the USPHS insignia as he addressed the group with a primary message for hospital administrators. He broke the news that all communication would be sent directly to the nurse directors of the schools of nursing. Each nursing school would need its own budget for audit purposes, a drastic change for many schools of nursing during the '40s. Budgets often lay buried within hospital expenditures controlled by the hospital board of directors. Tom always told the hospital administrators he knew he could count on their full cooperation, thus setting the stage for the rest of the meeting.

Then Tom asked for questions. Hands flew up at once and many expressed concerns about their schools of nursing. I stepped up to the podium and explained the issues and tasks that needed to be accomplished. Tom was always relieved that I could answer their questions.

Q. How was the goal of increasing the quantity and quality of nursing services with the Cadet Nurse Corps accomplished?

A. I give full credit to the 25 USPHS nurse education consultants who served in six regions throughout the country. These committed professional nurses worked hard and put in long hours. The consultants conducted Saturday morning workshops and invited all nurse educators in the area to participate. During these sessions they discussed and shared new and better ways to teach nursing students.

Nurse education consultants became the link between the USPHS and the schools of nursing, guiding directors and nurse educators in expanding and improving their curricula. Thus the nurse crisis on the home front was averted and nursing education improved because of the United States Cadet Nurse Corps.

References

Amidon, B. (1941). **Better nursing for America** (Public Affairs Pamphlet No. 10). (RG 90). Washington, DC: National Archives and Records Administration.

Cadet nurse sponsors California ship launching. (1945, April). **Cadet Nurse Corps News, 1, p. 3.** (Cadet Nurse File). Bethesda, MD: National Library of Medicine.

Dille, J. (Ed.). (1968). The president speaks. **Time capsule 1941: A history of the year.** (pp. 9-10). New York: Time/Life Books.

Nurse Training Program (1943). Public Law 74. 78th Congress, 1st session.

Nursing council on national defense (1940). **American Journal of Nursing, 40(9),** 1013.

Parran, T. (1943, August). Way clear to undertake vast cooperative program for training of nurse corps. **Hospitals.** pp. 29-30.

President Roosevelt to the American people. (Excerpt from the President's message to the people on December 7, 1941). (1942). **American Journal of Nursing, 42(1),** 16.

Stewart, I.M. (1940). Nursing education and national defense. **American Journal of Nursing, 40(12),** 1382.

Stewart, I.M. (1941). Nurse preparedness: Some lessons from World War I. **American Journal of Nursing, 41(7),** 804-815.

The national survey. (1941). **American Journal of Nursing, 41(2),** 929-930.

United States Federal Security Agency. (1950). The U.S. cadet nurse corps 1943-1948. (PHS Publication No. 38, pp.13-20; 97). Washington, DC: U.S. Government Printing Office.

Wartime nursing is different. (1943). **American Journal of Nursing, 43(9),** 835-838.

When does the home front have priority? (1943). **Public Health Nursing, 35(1),** 77-78.

2

Doing the Remarkable
by Paulie M. Perry

I talked to myself before you came, all this past week, and I said, Johnson, just don't tell everything. It was so bad; just don't tell everything. Tell a few things, because if you tell how it really was, hardly anyone would believe you, the way it was. I hardly believed it myself and I was there and saw it with my own eyes (R. Johnson, personal communication, May 27, 1995).

Ruth L. Johnson, was a tall, slim, witty former consultant for the USPHS. This was my first face-to-face meeting with a nurse education consultant of the U.S. Cadet Nurse Corps. I had spoken on the telephone with her and also with three other consultants who chose to remain anonymous. These giants in the nursing profession, now in their 80s and 90s, provided an essential link between the Corps and the schools of nursing across the nation.

I soon felt at ease with Nurse Educator Johnson in the living room of her spacious apartment at a retirement center in Norfolk, Nebraska. I had come to get her views of the Corps and to learn about her experiences with the implementation of the Corps.

What a privilege to interview her, for as she put it, "All of these people are dying off and one of these days there will be nobody left to tell the story."

The USPHS sought the best nurses they could find to administer the nurse-training programs, recruiting from the top positions in the country's leading schools of nursing. To participate in the Corps program, a school of nursing had to meet minimum requirements of the Corps. It was the responsibility of the nurse education consultants to visit and evaluate these schools. In the '40s only a few nursing schools had applied for professional accreditation so the consultant's visit was a first appraisal for many schools of nursing (Kalisch & Kalisch, 1975).

"Some of the schools were horrible; we closed them," said Johnson admitting it was a sore point with many. "If they couldn't get money to pay their students they wouldn't have any, and they might as well close. Some schools had to do that" (R. Johnson, personal communication, May 27, 1995).

The Division of Education decentralized its operations into six districts, each with at least one nurse education consultant, one public relations representative, and one auditor. The first district office opened in New Orleans, June 1944, and the others opened shortly thereafter in Richmond, Virginia; New York City; San Francisco; Chicago; and Kansas City, Missouri. Twenty-five consultants assigned throughout the United States used their expertise to assist over 1,000 schools of nursing with recruitment, the senior cadet experience, and the accelerated program (U.S. Federal Security Agency, 1950).

The nurse education consultants visited the schools to ascertain the quality and number of instructional personnel and the clinical facilities. They also reviewed the curricula, the weekly schedule of hours, and the health and guidance programs. The consultants determined if the school complied with the requirement for acceleration of the program, and if the optimal number of students was enrolled. Both of these areas were critical factors in relieving the nursing shortage. According to Consultant Johnson, "We observed their programs of instruction because what they reported on paper wasn't necessarily what they did" (R. Johnson, personal communication, May 27, 1995).

Another consultant said:

> Before visiting a school, I first went over its application, noting especially the financial part. I wrote the directors of the state board

of nurse examiners giving each a tentative schedule of the visits I would make in their state. I invited the state board's director to meet with me at any of the locations and often the director did. At other times they met with me in the evening for dinner. It was necessary for the federal and state agencies to work together because the standards of state boards of nurse examiners varied widely from state to state, which was a concern for the consultants. Also, with the accelerated program of the Corps, graduating cadets had to meet the requirements of their licensing agency.

We emphasized education for the students. Realistically, staffing of the hospital by cadet nurses was a priority due to the shortage of personnel during the national emergency. However, we consultants helped nurse directors visualize the path nursing would need to take after the war. I used my influence with the hospital administrators to push for needed improvements in the school programs. Often these problems or deficiencies, ignored by administrators for years, were ones that the directors of the programs recognized but could not change.

The nurse education consultants frequently were faced with animosity when they confronted school of nursing representatives about irregularities in their programs. In a visit to a school of nursing another consultant discovered that the physician-administrator wanted to use the Cadet Nurse Corps funds for hospital services. She informed him that cadet funds had to be used for nurse education. The administrator became angry but failed to intimidate the petite and feisty consultant. The young, timid director of nursing who attended the meeting asked the consultant, "How did you stand up to him like that?"

Sometimes a director of nursing felt threatened by a consultant's visit. As Consultant Johnson stated, "When I told the director what was wrong with the program I used the approach that the school of nursing could correct the problem and do better. You couldn't tell the director how bad it was without giving them help to fix it, but it was tough" (R. Johnson, personal communication, May 27, 1995).

The auditors followed up on the consultants' reports. A school could receive conditional approval with a 3-, 6-, or 12-month probation period to bring the school to Corps standards.

This time period gave the school an opportunity to plan for the necessary improvements and prove their good intentions. It also provided the consultants with added clout. If funds were taken away, and if the public media learned about this information, the publicity could be devastating not only to the school of nursing but to the hospital as well. However, the USPHS preferred working with schools of nursing rather than having open conflict with them, and withdrawal of funds was kept quiet in the worst cases.

In one instance, a consultant had to confront two physicians who were both the owners and administrators of the hospital and the associated school of nursing. Their program did not meet the requirements of the Corps in certain areas. These discrepancies were reported. The surgeon general received a telephone call from the senior senator of the state where the hospital at fault was located challenging the findings. According to the consultant, "I tell you with pride that the surgeon general backed up my report. Things had to change or the money would be held up. It had to be [that way] because they didn't meet the requirements."

The nurse education consultants in uniform with the USPHS insignia gave direct and specific service to the schools of nursing in their districts. They traveled hundreds of miles and wrote thousands of letters to become familiar with all the university and hospital schools of nursing.

Sometimes traveling in wartime could be a challenge. According to Consultant Johnson:

> Since I lived in Chicago prior to going with the Cadet Nurse Corps, I knew it well and I think that is the reason they gave me this area. The travel in and out of Chicago was easier than in lots of places, with good accommodations by train or bus. However, many times I reached my destination late in the day and because of the war, my hotel room was released to another person. I slept in all kinds of peculiar places (R. Johnson, personal communication, May 27, 1995).

Sometimes a consultant went to the airport to catch an airplane only to find that the plane could not arrive because of dust or snowstorms. This threw her schedule off because all her appointments hinged on the first visit. Often the trains did not leave on time; troop trains moving military service personnel across the country had priority over trains carrying civilians. The consultant's situation changed when she got a car.

When the government finally provided me with a small car, a Willis, I could arrive at my destination the night before my appointment and keep my itinerary.

On one of my trips I checked in at the local hotel and discovered my reservation had been given to an earlier arrival. I didn't know what to do, so I called the commanding officer at the Army air base and told him of my plight and asked if I could stay on the base overnight. He hemmed and hawed but finally said yes.

Looking very professional in my officer's uniform I went to the base and found I was the only woman among thousands of servicemen. A soldier took me to a small portable structure that had a wooden base and a tent-top. Inside he showed me a freshly made bed and said it was where I was to sleep.

During the night I heard footsteps and peeked out the window to see a sentry patrolling around the shelter. I got up early in the morning and left before breakfast. I should have waited and paid my compliments to the commanding officer but I sent him a note instead.

In their examinations of facilities, consultants discovered some unusual situations. In one school a consultant asked to see the laboratory and found it consisted of a single Bunsen burner in the basement.

Another time a consultant visited a seemingly satisfactory school in an area deluged with rain. She asked to visit the library.

They took me to the basement where I had to walk across a plank because of the foot-deep water on the floor of the library. The planks had been placed on the second-shelf level from one side of the room to the other. Fortunately none of the books were under water but the school had to get themselves a suitable library.

She also found that libraries were often poor in smaller schools so she provided a library list to schools of nursing to assist them in choosing reference books.

On one occasion a consultant found what she was not looking for when she checked housing facilities of the schools of nursing for cleanliness, safety, number of bathrooms, and quality of food. As the consultant stated:

> I went through a lovely, new nurses' residence and thought, my goodness these cadets have a tremendous number of clothes. The closets are full. I became suspicious and discovered that the school had twice as many cadets as beds. The cadets took turns using the beds, sleeping in shifts. I told the director this would not do and that they had to rent rooms in town for their senior students. I'm sure the auditors followed up on that report.

On a visit to one of the schools, Consultant Johnson got on the hotel elevator to go down to breakfast and discovered Surgeon General Parran there. She was surprised to see him. They went into the coffee shop where Dr. Parran asked her to tell him about the visit. She replied by saying, "Well I don't think I'll tell you everything because we're eating breakfast." On a previous visit the hospital administrator had berated Johnson in a torrent of harsh words because of her report listing the school's failings. Johnson knew he had complained to Dr. Parran about her inspection. However she told Dr. Parran the details of the confrontation with the superintendent except for one detail. She didn't tell him that while the corpulent superintendent poured out his tirade on her, he sat spread-legged with his fly open (R. Johnson, personal communication, May 27, 1995).

Visits to schools of nursing also had their bright moments for the nurse education consultants. One aspect of the job some consultants liked best was talking with the cadets. Others found great satisfaction in meeting with the school administrators and using these opportunities to suggest improvements in the school's program. One consultant was gratified to see the elevation of hospital standards of operation in the facilities and their affiliations with colleges and universities.

A highlight of one consultant's career was a visit by General Eisenhower, the hero of V-E (Victory in Europe) Day to a city in her area. All the military, in full uniform, sweltered as they waited for his noon arrival at the train station on an unmercifully hot day. One of the naval officers from the nearby base said, "I hope we don't have to stand and salute as General Eisenhower comes out onto the platform, because staying in that position a few minutes might make the women in uniform feel faint." The consultant wondered why he thought the men would be exempt from fainting.

Finally the train arrived and General "Ike" came out onto the platform, whipped off his cap put it under his arm and waved. The military gratefully assumed an "at ease" stature and no one fainted.

A public relations (PR) person in the office of one of the consultants discovered that part of General Ike's homecoming

Welcome home, Ike! In July 1945 cheering cadet nurses and others in Abilene, Kansas, welcomed General Dwight D. Eisenhower after V-E (Victory in Europe) Day. Crowds honored Ike as the leader of the victorious Allied armies and as the representative of men and women who served with him.

would include a visit to his mother in a nearby city. The PR representative knew the route the motor entourage would take and arranged for cadet nurses to be at the spot where the car would slow to a stop. The car, a great, long vehicle with no top for protection from the hot sun, was parked at the specified time and place. As coached by the PR person, the cadets came up to both sides of the car to greet the celebrated general. The photographer alerted by the PR person kept his camera flashing. The picture of General Eisenhower surrounded by cadet nurses received national coverage and greatly pleased the USPHS office in Washington. Of course all those in the district office were doubly delighted because these cadets were from their area.

Although the nurse education consultants had little or no previous experience in government, they plunged into the administration of the U.S. Cadet Nurse Corps with enthusiasm and high morale. These pioneers in a project that linked government with private industry felt pride and satisfaction in being a part of a unified effort of such great national significance.

The consultants attributed the success of the Corps in large part to Director Lucile Petry. One described Director Petry as a "Woman of Vision." The consultants saw much improvement in the administration and curriculum of the schools of nursing with the advent of the Corps and believed this would not have happened if Director Petry had not been at the helm of the program.

Corps Director Lucile Petry praised the nurse education consultants in their valuable roles as interpreters. The consultants interpreted all aspects of the U.S. Cadet Nurse Corps to the participating schools of nursing. Consultants also translated school of nursing programs to the USPHS. In doing this, they linked the two and personalized the relationship. As Lucile Petry said, "It is the desire of the nurse education consultant to help schools maintain and raise standards by advising and assisting them in solving problems caused by war-created shortages (1945, p. 807).

An account of the Corps would not be complete without input from the directors of nursing and nurse educators. The following question and the answer from a director of nursing at a Midwest hospital school of nursing provide a more complete picture.

Q. What effects did the Cadet Nurse Corps have on the schools of nursing, their programs, and on nursing in general?

A. My experiences with the Cadet Nurse Corps left me with a negative attitude. I had full responsibility for carrying out the directives of the Cadet Nurse Corps. To accommodate the increased number of students, the school of nursing rented three houses near the hospital and procured another housemother. Another challenge included finding and keeping good faculty. I worked long hours, sometimes up to 14 hours a day in my office, with only 1 day off each week.

For this director, the U.S. Cadet Nurse Corps was a big headache. The Corps required extensive record keeping and a complete accounting of all the uniforms. She also had full responsibility for managing the government funding because the hospital bookkeeper refused to do it. On the positive side, she said her brother was serving in the South Pacific and that she wanted to support him and the war effort. "I lived in the nurses' home, thankful I could walk to my room at night and not be afraid of the Japanese and could have a hot bath."

Although the Corps brought more students to the school, wartime meant fewer faculty were available because many left to follow their servicemen. At a time when the director needed nurses desperately, she had to let a percentage of her senior cadets go to work in other hospitals. According to this director, "Only one cadet said the 6-months' senior experience was an advantage to her ... she found her husband in the other hospital."

On the other hand, an instructor from another Midwest school of nursing told of her excitement when she learned about the Corps. She urged the hospital superintendent to take advantage of the opportunity. According to her:

The faculty's dreams were realized. The school acquired an anatomical model of the body, replacing the woebegone skeleton. We obtained new charts, enlarged the library and finally had a sufficient quantity of beds, linen, and "Mrs. Chase" mannequins for students to practice nursing arts procedures. The school of nursing classes of 15 students more than doubled and the hospital purchased homes in the neighborhood to house the cadets.

The hospital, which was still in financial trouble from the Depression, paid off its debt and began to plan for expansion. The hospital continued in its growth to become a well-known medical facility, and the school of nursing linked its 3-year program with a neighboring university.

Summary

The USPHS Nurse Education Consultants provided the link between the surgeon general's office in Washington, D.C., and more than 1,000 schools of nursing. The efforts of the consultants, the directors of nursing, and the nurse instructors came alive in the thousands of cadets who came from hamlets, cities, and farms across the United States. Using cadet nurses to solve a critical nurse shortage while also raising the standards for educating nurses was a remarkable accomplishment.

References

Kalisch, B.J., & Kalisch, P.A. (1975). Slaves, servants, or saints? An analysis of the system of nurse training in the United States 1873-1948. Nursing Forum, 14(3), 253-258.
Petry, L. (1945). Duties of nurse education consultants. American Journal of Nursing, 45(10), 807.
United States Federal Security Agency. (1950). The U.S. Cadet Nurse Corps 1943-1948. (PHS Publication No.38, p. 68). Washington, DC: U.S. Government Printing Office.

3

We Joined the Cadets
by Paulie M. Perry

As a kid I envied cats because mother held and patted them but not us kids. Mother was ill with tuberculosis and hoped to keep us children from being contaminated but we were all exposed anyhow (Charlotte Allen Rogers).

Charlotte grew up in rural America as did many cadet nurses. Cadet nurses came into the Corps from the hills of West Virginia, the Cascades of the Northwest, and from the prairie states stretching from the Dakotas to Texas. Searching for an education, many cadets did not realize the effect they had on nursing during World War II and the postwar years.

The following cadet nurse stories provide background information about the young people who joined the U S. Cadet Nurse Corps and the events that moved them toward a career in nursing. Charlotte Rogers' story about how she became a cadet nurse is a good place to begin. When Charlotte was a baby in the back hills of West Virginia, her sick mother had a pulmonary hemorrhage and received treatment at a tuberculosis (TB) sanitarium at Terre Haute, Indiana. Charlotte lived with neighbors from that time until her third birthday. Her father then sent her to boarding school for 3 years to separate her from her contagious mother. She had to ride the caboose on the logging train until it reached the junction where she transferred to the passenger train. Charlotte remembers the smell of the exhaust always made her feel sick.

Then came the Depression. Banks failed, the Allen family suffered financial distress, and the children had to attend the three-room school near home. However, they preferred this to the strictly run Roman Catholic boarding school.

From the age of 12, Charlotte took care of her mother, who often coughed and coughed until she hemorrhaged. As Charlotte stated:

> I learned about contagion while caring for mother by boiling dishes and burning contaminated bundles. At 13, I stayed out of school a full year to care for mother and my new baby brother so my sister could finish high school.

> When war came to Europe, I told my father I would volunteer for nursing if the United States got involved. Since I had been a primary care giver for a family member, it was natural for me to choose nursing. My family thought this was a wise choice.

> After Pearl Harbor I actively pursued a nursing career. I visited my sister, a student at St. Mary's School of Nursing at Huntington, West Virginia, and found the school had openings in its February 1942 class. I had enough credits to apply even though I had not yet graduated from high school.

> I sent a transcript to the school and received an acceptance with the additional good news that the school awarded a $50 scholarship. This money paid for my books and the school furnished my uniforms, board, and room. I joined the Cadet Nurse Corps in 1943 with the first inductees. It was a lifesaver for me because I had no money.

Geraldine D'Olivo Sawyer, who was born and raised in Tacoma, Washington, remembered her reasons for becoming a cadet nurse. Like Charlotte, she was a middle child whose mother had a disabling physical condition. Geraldine's older sister died of polio at the age of 3. Her mother served on many city committees and helped pioneer the provision of restroom areas for the disabled. Because of an injury as a child, her mother used crutches. Geraldine told her story as follows:

> From the time I read my first Sue Barton nurse-series book in the '30s, I wanted to be a nurse. I believed this would fulfill a prerequisite to be an airline stewardess, a much glamorized role in the movies.

However, because I was just over 5 feet tall, I did not meet the minimum height requirement so being a stewardess was out.

After December 7th, I wished I were older and a graduate nurse so I could join the Armed Forces. However, my parents supported my decision to pursue nursing. My father encouraged the professions for his children and my mother, an art teacher, wanted me to be happy in my decision. As a high school senior I wrote to universities and schools of nursing from Washington to California for information on their programs.

A good friend, a senior in nursing, told me about the Cadet Nurse Corps. I joined the Corps after entering the Tacoma General Hospital School of Nursing. My parents would have helped me attain my nursing career even without the Corps. They believed in the importance of education.

Ellen Justice Perkins and her sisters grew up in the Salvation Army Orphanage in Greenville, South Carolina. Ellen, Helen, and Evelyn were triplets and attended public schools. The church organized youth activities and held services in the

ELLEN JUSTICE PERKINS COLLECTION

Helen, Evelyn, and Ellen Justice (left to right), inspired by Salvation Army "Ladies in White," chose nursing as a career and entered Roanoke (Virginia) Memorial Hospital School of Nursing. They constituted half of the special June 1944 U.S. Cadet Nurse Corps class, which was later merged with the fall class of 18.

orphanage or local Army hall. The community helped the 60-some boys and girls who lived at the orphanage enjoy life. The auxiliary sponsored trips, an annual 4th of July picnic, and monthly birthday parties. Nothing surpassed a trip to the circus or a fair.

Ellen's path to the Corps was strongly influenced by these early activities. Her story indicates that influence.

Being surrounded by the Salvation Army "ladies in white" from early childhood influenced my choice to be a nurse. The superintendent's daughter and one of the officers on the staff were RNs. My sisters and I often plied them with questions about nursing, such as, "How do you turn a mattress with the patient in the bed?" They would show us how it could be done.

The staff at the Home did not think we could make it into nursing school because of our grades. But our desire to become nurses prevailed. We took postgraduate high school courses to complete the required subjects. Our plans to become nurses were put on hold when we joined the ranks of the Salvation Army for a 5-year stint. I served in the Home and Hospital for Unwed Mothers in Louisville, Kentucky; Evelyn served in a similar home in Roanoke, Virginia; and Helen fulfilled her obligation in the day nursery in Baltimore, Maryland.

My sisters and I wanted to go to the same nursing school. [We were] stationed far apart, [so] we depended on the U.S. mail for communication. Letters flew back and forth [among] Louisville, Baltimore, and Roanoke. We finally agreed upon the Roanoke Memorial Hospital in Virginia as the first choice for our school of nursing.

Because the Cadet Nurse Corps urged schools of nursing to increase enrollments, Roanoke Memorial Hospital created a special June class and accepted us. We made up half of the class of cadet nurses, which later merged with the fall class of 18.

I learned about the Cadet Nurse Corps from the radio, the newspaper, magazines, and word of mouth. Through its financial support, I fulfilled my dream to become a Registered Nurse. The Cadet Nurse Corps gave my sisters and me an opportunity in nursing that we would not have had otherwise.

Another story about how the Cadet Nurse Corps helped a young woman become a nurse is told by Pertronella Buck Arledge who grew up in a small farming community in Texas. Pertronella, too, was able to get an education and to enter a career in nursing because of the Corps' financial support.

When I was 10 years old, my family moved from Waxahachie, Texas, to Buena Vista, 6 miles away. We adjusted to this difficult move made necessary because of the lack of jobs for father in town. He leased a small farm and raised much of our food. Unlike many families, we did not go hungry. My grandfather loaned my father his farm equipment and livestock. The farmhouse, a dilapidated shack, had no running water or indoor plumbing. With fortitude and determination we survived.

The hard times of the 1930s influenced my becoming a nurse. The most likely careers for women at the time were teaching, secretarial work, or nursing. In my case nursing won by a landslide. Seeing the poverty all around me, I desired a career that would allow me to make a good living for myself. I did not want to spend my life around a cotton patch. Empathy for those in need was always a strong interest of mine.

When I was in the 9th grade, I wrote to a nursing school in Dallas for information. I nearly wore out their brochure looking at it and dreaming about the day when I could go there to become a nurse.

After high school graduation my mother took me for an interview at the Dallas school. The director looked me over and talked with me, but it was not a positive experience. The director told mother and me that the school did not accept applicants until they were 18 and that I should go home, grow up, then come back. The disappointment was indescribable. I did grow up the next year but I did not do it at home.

I landed a job as a nurses' aide at Hillcrest Memorial Hospital in Waco, Texas. I lived in the basement of the hospital, worked 10-hour days, a 6 1/2 day week for which I received $15 a month plus board and room. I shared the room with four other girls.

Soon after employment as a nurses' aide, I learned that the hospital would be participating in the Cadet Nurse Corps program. I continued to work there until the school reopened in October 1943 after an 11-year closure. The nursing school made quick adjustments to qualify for participation in the Corps, erecting a dormitory, finding instructors, and turning a big house behind the hospital into an educational building.

My parents strongly supported my decision to go into nursing. Being patriotic and having only daughters, it pleased them that I wanted to join the Cadet Nurse Corps and contribute to the war effort. An aunt tried to discourage me by telling me my only duty would be emptying bedpans. That comment only increased the spark in me to go ahead with my plans. I wanted to find out about nursing on my own, but my parents could not financially provide a nursing education. So the Cadet Nurse Corps afforded an opportunity I would not have had otherwise.

In another part of the country and during the Depression another young girl, Dorothy Luther, found her way into the Corps to become a nurse. Unlike Ellen and Petronella, Dorothy had no early aspirations of becoming a nurse. But she discovered that she enjoyed work as a volunteer nurses' aide and that she could get an education at a prestigious university as a member of the Corps. In Dorothy's words:

My earliest recollection was living in an upstairs, one-bedroom apartment in a four-unit apartment building in Coral Gables, Florida. My family, consisting of a mother, father, and a brother 6 years older than me, moved to Miami from Boston in 1926.

My father and uncle had grand ideas of making "gobs" of money in Florida real estate as others had reportedly done. When their dreams failed to materialize my father found employment with the Southern Bell telephone company, from which he eventually retired with 47 years of service.

Coral Gables, a well-to-do suburb west of Miami, was one of the first planned cities in the United States. My family lived rent-free in exchange for my dad's management of the apartment building and grounds. My parents slept in the bedroom, my brother on the screened-in porch and I had the "Murphy" bed in the living room.

On sunny days a rooftop black solar system heated the water. On rainy days we heated the water on the stove. Except for a similar building behind ours, we were surrounded by several blocks of vacant lots, all with sidewalks, which were marvelous for roller-skating.

Those were the Depression years. My mother sewed beautifully and made most of my clothes. She also operated a sewing shop in the business district. She sent linens to the laundry but hand washed most of our clothing. The iceman delivered a 25-pound block of ice every other day for the icebox and a man made rounds once a year to sharpen knives and scissors. My brother managed a Saturday Evening Post delivery route and my father bred and raised rabbits. When the young bunnies reached 2 to 3 pounds, he dressed them out [for cooking] and sold them to his colleagues at the office.

After graduating from high school but with no financial means to attend college, I accepted a position as bookkeeper and payroll clerk for a venetian blind company. I served as a volunteer for the U.S. Army Interceptor Command in Miami whose mission consisted of identifying and plotting air traffic along the east coast of Florida. The command post closed when the Allied offensive escalated.

Desiring to continue to help in the war effort, I enrolled in a Red Cross nurses' aide training course at the county hospital. After 250 hours of clinical work I earned a pin and served as a volunteer in the evening. To my surprise I thoroughly enjoyed the work and, needing a challenge, decided to make nursing a career. The Cadet Nurse Corps made it possible for me to enroll at the Duke University School of Nursing in Durham, North Carolina, from which I graduated in 1948.

In a Philadelphia neighborhood of blue- and white-collar workers, another young girl found the pathway to nursing via the cadet corps. Florence Blake Ford, the daughter of parents who had emigrated from England and Wales, did not always want to be a nurse. In fact, it was purely a decision of convenience that she entered the Corps. Her story follows:

Father volunteered as an air-raid warden and took a first-aid course while mother knitted socks for Bundles for Britain and rolled Red Cross bandages. The family also supported the British War Relief fundraisers.

I was an avid reader and took commercial courses so I would have a skill after high school graduation. My parents, having been sent to work at age 14, did not have the money or the inclination to stress education beyond high school.

When I was visiting a friend in the hospital, I saw a poster inviting me to become a cadet nurse and obtain an education-free. The light went on. Here was a way for me to escape from my boring clerical job and obtain an education in another field. I went for an interview at the school of nursing; they agreed to take me on probation, with the provision that I take algebra and a science course that summer of 1945.

The day after VJ Day I went to the Methodist Hospital School of Nursing in Philadelphia to inquire if the Cadet Nurse Corps was still viable. Thank God it was. My parents supported my decision to become a nurse. My father was particularly pleased because his mother's family worked on the Verney estates in England where Florence Nightingale often resided. His mother, a namesake of Miss Nightingale, named a daughter Florence, then I became the third generation to bear Miss Nightingale's name.

Frankly I jumped at the opportunity to become a cadet nurse because it was free, and if I completed the course I could earn more money than I currently made as a clerk. This decision of convenience turned out to be a decision "made in heaven." I loved nursing.

My own story of going into the cadet nurse corps was one of sister following sister and the impression the Corps made on those of us who had an interest in nursing but lacked the funds to pursue it.

What took me from our Morey farm in Kansas to the Cadet Nursing Corps was my sister. Thelma Morey Robinson entered nurses' training and became a cadet nurse. I was impressed with my tour of Lincoln General Hospital and nurses' residence. Attending her candlelight capping ceremony confirmed my decision that I wanted a nursing career. Mother had concern for my health, since the nurses she knew worked long hours, often around the clock. She told me that nursing could break my health. My parents, however, gave their sanction without question. Thelma had already convinced them that nursing was an acceptable and noble profession and the Cadet Nurse Corps made it affordable as well. Which school of nursing was for me? My sister's school, Lincoln General Hospital School of Nursing, of course!

In 1943 Thelma Morey (left) enrolled at Lincoln (Nebraska) General Hospital School of Nursing. She became Paulie Morey's "big sister" at the school when Paulie enrolled in 1945. Both were members of the U.S. Cadet Nurse Corps.

4

A Lifetime Education—Free
by Thelma M. Robinson

Young lady, if you get lonesome don't come home crying, as this is entirely your decision.

These parting words of Donna Rae Hardenburger Kennedy's father stung when she left home in north central Kansas and boarded the bus for the 90-mile ride to Lincoln, Nebraska, in September 1944. Donna Rae, my sister Paulie's and my childhood friend, had written me asking about life as a cadet nurse. Now a junior cadet, I could answer her questions, which I did and I also drew a picture of the uniform that would distinguish her as a student at Lincoln General Hospital School of Nursing.

Donna Rae recalled that her parents wanted her to be a teacher. In their opinion, only "bad" girls were nurses. In the '40s, some people believed that nurses, who knew so much about the human body were "loose" women. But Donna Rae's persistence won her parents over, and she became a nurse.

Jean Henderson, chief of recruitment and public relations for the U.S. Cadet Nurse Corps, recognized parental negative beliefs about nurses. Mothers considered nursing to be degrading, backbreaking work. Fathers thought board, room, and a small salary was inadequate compensation for the rigorous demands of professional nurses. Ms. Henderson feared these negative parental reactions could prevent 17- and

18-year-old women from doing something that would be of personal benefit as well as a war service (Henderson, 1945).

Before the war, the growing demand for nurses had not been met. Now with the war raging, the need for nurses was even more urgent. Could a sufficient number of qualified young women be recruited to enter nursing in time to prevent a crisis?

The U.S. Cadet Nurse Corps quota called for 65,000 new student nurses during the first year, almost twice the number admitted to schools of nursing during peacetime. Complex attitudes about student nurses and nursing confronted Jean Henderson when she initiated the recruitment campaign for cadet nurses (U.S. War Advertising Council/ Office of War Information/USPHS).

Before the U.S. Cadet Nurse Corps existed, nurses received little attention from the media. Like physicians and certain other professionals, nurses shied away from publicity, viewing it as unprofessional, unethical, and undignified. In addition, nurses often lacked the skills necessary to present themselves and their cause effectively. Now Jean set out to bombard the country with appeals designed to persuade the country about the need for student nurses, emphasizing that nursing was a respected profession (Kalisch & Kalisch, 1973).

The USPHS, with Jean Henderson at the helm of cadet nurse recruitment, worked closely with the Office of War Information (OWI). The recruitment of women into war production and services was one of the major projects of OWI.

The USPHS and OWI compiled guidelines and suggestions for advertisers to use. Themes such as "War Work Now," "Scholarships for Complete Education," and "Nursing-A Design for a Successful Homemaking or Professional Career," dramatized the urgent need for young women to enter the nursing profession (USOWI, 1945).

According to OWI's publicity promotion, being a nurse called for personal sacrifice and an unselfish dedication to humanitarian work, a sacrifice that only the finest type of woman could fulfill. Still, some parents worried that the Corps would take their daughters out of circulation. But the persistent

OWI declared that the marriage rate was unusually high among nurses. Nurses made good wives, mothers, and community leaders.

The OWI worked closely with the War Advertising Council. This voluntary organization, made up of major advertising companies, donated services and publicized important war causes. Thousands of people contributed time and space for publicity. Advertisers donated $13 million of services, utilizing all available media to attract unprecedented numbers of new students into nursing within a short time (U.S. Office of War Information/Division of Nurse Education, 1945).

The USPHS welcomed certain advertisers to become sponsors of the U.S. Cadet Nurse Corps recruitment campaign. Appropriate products and services listed for the cooperative advertising scheme included: pharmaceuticals, insurance, public utilities, heavy industries, and such products as cosmetics, food, household equipment, and women's wear. Cigarette and alcohol companies were not asked to be sponsors.

WOMEN IN MILITARY SERVICE FOR AMERICA MEMORIAL FOUNDATION

Cadet nurse Evelyn Gahm, second from left, and her sisters Ellen (WAC), Dorothy (Marine Corps), and Florence (WAVE) were welcomed home fall 1945 by their parents in Boulder, Colorado, where they celebrated the end of World War II.

(U.S. Division of Nurse Education/Federal Security Agency/ USPHS, 1944).

Companies by the hundreds came forth with inspiration showing nursing as women's war work. The Eastman Kodak Company promoted the U.S. Cadet Nurse Corps in a full-page color advertisement ("Advertising News and Notes," 1944). The benefits to 17- and 18-year-old young women who joined the Corps were announced in 15 leading national magazines. High school graduates interested in nursing were directed to write to Box 88, New York, NY, for information. At this address the National Nursing Council for War Service received about 23,000 inquires during May and June 1943 ("War Activities," 1943).

But the best of efforts sometimes backfire. The surgeon general's office received word that the U.S. Cadet Nurses Corps had a cooperative advertisement with Southern Comfort. Dr. Parran asked Director Lucile Petry to check on this information. Petry called the publicist in that region, who confessed that she didn't know Southern Comfort was a whiskey; she said she thought it was a mattress ("Cadet Nurse Corps Anniversary," 1994). All types of public news media cooperated in the recruitment of cadet nurses. Moviegoers watched news clips of President Roosevelt signing the Bolton Act; another news clip featured a display of the cadet nurse corps uniform at the Waldorf Astoria Hotel. "Reward Unlimited," produced by Vanguard Films, starred Dorothy McGuire as a young woman who joined the cadets. This motion picture won an award as the best women's war recruitment film for 1944 (Kalisch & Kalisch, 1973).

Articles about the Corps appeared in such magazines as *Mademoiselle, Cornet, Charm, Rotarian,* and a host of others. An article entitled, "Wanted: Cadet Nurses" made this appeal to the subscribers of the magazine, *Parents*:

> One out of every 10 girls graduating from high school during 1944 must begin nurses' training if the country's health is to be safeguarded. Thousands of nurses are serving in the Army and Navy;

thousands more must join the armed forces this year ... hospitals, industrial plants, and social services are woefully understaffed. The demand for nursing skill will not end with the war. When peace comes, not only our country but the whole world will need the graduate nurse's wisdom, courage, and skill ("Wanted: Cadet Nurses," 1944, p. 40).

Cadet nurses appeared on the covers of the *Ladies Home Journal, Harper's Bazaar, Colliers,* and *Scholastic Magazine.* Cadet nurse cover girls and magazine stories convinced Dorothy Preusser Ringsbach to join the Corps. She said, "When I saw magazine pictures of cadet nurses, I thought, 'What a way to go. With the war on, this was one way I could serve my country, get an education, and wear that beautiful uniform.'"

The private sector helped the high-powered recruitment appeal aimed primarily at high-school girls nearing graduation. Groups volunteering on behalf of the Corps included:

- Parent Teacher Associations
- Rotary International
- Daughters of the American Revolution
- Kiwanis
- Lions
- Auxiliary of the American Legion
- Fraternal Order of the Moose
- Elks
- General Federation of Women's Clubs

These groups distributed recruitment materials and persuaded girls in their communities to join the Corps (Henderson, 1945).

Posters with the message, "Enlist in a Proud Profession: Get a Lifetime Education—Free!" urged young women to join the U.S. Cadet Nurse Corps. Millions of colorful placards placed in theater lobbies, women's shoe stores, beauty shops, high schools, libraries, YWCAs, and churches proclaimed that girls had a future in nursing.

A cadet nurse recruitment poster with a pretty girl looking smart in a gray beret and uniform captivated the attention of

Dorothie Melvin Crowley, a recent high school graduate. She thought joining the Corps would be a great way for her to serve during the war. She said:

> My best friend and I wrote to Box 88 in New York for information on how to become that "smart looking girl" on the poster. My mother didn't approve and thought I would become a well trained servant. My father, who was happy that I wanted to be a nurse, secretly hoped I would be a doctor or a nurse. He worried that if he said too much about it, I would balk at the idea.
>
> As a young man my father worked with the family doctor after high school. The doctor thought he was interested in medicine and had a great potential. He planned to finance Dad's education. However, the doctor died before this could happen. Dad's parents wanted him to go into the family business, a photography and recording studio. They didn't want him in the medical field, and the family probably couldn't afford it. So I made Daddy happy when I chose nursing.

The cadet nurse message was broadcast on radio soap operas, variety shows, symphony concerts, and documentaries. The popular radio show, "One Man's Family," added a cadet nurse to the serial. Dorothy Preusser Ringlesbach's sister worked for local radio station, WOWO, in Fort Wayne, Indiana, and arranged for Dorothy to describe for the radio audience the cadet nurse uniform she was wearing and tell what the Corps offered.

Cadets themselves were considered to be the best recruiters. The Cadet Nurse Corps News, the official paper for the Corps, published this information:

> We hope you will polish up your buttons, don your trim gray and scarlet, and tell your friends about the Corps.... Stress the fact that futures in nursing are rainbow bright-either as preparation for homemaking or as a career in itself. Say, too, that enrollment in the Corps 90 days before the end of the war entitles a cadet nurse to complete her nurse education under a federal scholarship ("One Good Cadet Recruits Another," 1945, p. 3).

Margaret Reagan, publicity chair for the Recruitment Committee of the Minneapolis Nursing Council of War Service, approached the General Outdoor Advertising Company of that city with an idea ("Minnesota Cadet Nurse Corps Campaign," 1944). She suggested a billboard campaign to promote the recruitment of cadet nurses, and asked a prominent nurse leader and a cadet nurse in uniform to help. Lucille Sanfranski Hickey recalled this unique experience:

> The uniform was great; gray is my color. Thrilled to be asked to model the uniform, I accompanied our superintendent of nurses on a tour of St. Paul's largest corporations to solicit money to buy billboard spaces to advertise the Corps. What a week-meeting important people and eating delicious lunches at popular cafes!

Cadet nurses and Dr. Thomas S. Parran, surgeon general of the U.S. Public Health Service, participated in a nationwide radio broadcast of the popular program, *We the People*.

Two hundred and seventy roadway signs featuring a cadet nurse appeared in prominent locations in Minneapolis, St. Paul, and Duluth, Minnesota. The promotional message was, "Enlist in a Proud Profession. Join the U.S. Cadet Nurse Corps. A Lifetime Education-Free-for high school graduates who qualify." As a result, many phone calls and letters were received by Minnesota schools of nursing from people inquiring about the Corps ("Minnesota Cadet Nurse Corps Campaign," 1944).

Other media also targeted high school students for recruitment into the Corps. A picture of student nurses in the classroom appeared on the cover of the teacher's edition of *Scholastic Magazine* (1944). A story, "So Proudly We Hail" began, "Today's $64 question for high school girls about to graduate is-where do I fit into the war picture?" Details about the Cadet Nurse Corps explained what the program offered.

Alice Jans Donley from South Dakota learned about the Corps in high school. The teachers in her small school kept students informed about what was going on in the world and of waiting opportunities.

High schools in other areas cooperated in the recruitment effort of young women. The Long Island Nursing Council in New York sent a speaker to each of the 132 high schools in that area and showed a film, "RN Serving All Mankind." Schools of nursing in Long Island held open houses and 2,000 high school students visited ("War Activities," 1943).

A sign, "Be a Cadet Nurse" intrigued Alice Chiastka Prendergast. Her parents were undertakers and she worked in their Chicago business as a bookkeeper, organist, and hairdresser-a Jill of all trades. Her mother was active in church, PTA, and women's clubs. Her sister was a ballerina and totally involved with show business-on the road frequently. Her brother worked in the funeral business. Alice excelled in school but college was not an option; "Come to work in our business," her family said.

Alice, a 28-year-old married woman with a husband serving in the Pacific, was not satisfied and wanted to be part of the war effort. With her secretarial background, she thought that if she joined the WAC or WAVES, she would wind up behind another typewriter. The Corps was her chance for a new career and she could fulfill her patriotic duty as well.

Her age and marital status worked against her being a candidate in great demand, despite her good scholastic record. The director of Michael Reese Hospital School of Nursing said they would consider her if she attained high scores on their 3-day, pre-entrance test. She did and they accepted her.

Young women began to learn about the Corps through a variety of channels. Mary Joan Harris Ray grew up on a farm in Kickapoo Valley, Wisconsin, and heard about the Corps at a county fair. In Gainsville, New York, the cleaning woman at the large office where Margaret Smith Fairbanks worked informed her about the Corps. Her son's girlfriend was a cadet nurse.

Student nurses already enrolled in a school of nursing who had at least 1 year remaining before they completed their programs were eligible to join the Corps. Lillian Dickow Brown, a junior at Columbia Hospital School of Nursing in Milwaukee, declined the offer. She said, "Being a young patriotic lady, I chose to remain at my present status, that of paying my own way. [I believed] the government had enough expenses waging the war."

The U.S. Cadet Nurse Corps proved to be one of the most successful and economical recruitment efforts of World War II. In the first year of recruitment the 65,000 cadet-nurse quota was exceeded by 521. Many cadet nurses, the first Corps members to graduate, enlisted in a military service. The Cadet Nurse Corps News (1945) published an article about the February 1945 graduating class of Grady Hospital School of Nursing in Atlanta, Georgia, and their 100% enrollment in military nurse corps.

On February 6, 1945, Surgeon General Thomas Parran reported to the House Committee on Military Affairs that approximately 10,500 cadet nurses graduated during the first 18 months, from the beginning in August 1943 through January 1945. Forty percent had applied to or had been accepted by the military service. The surgeon general reported cadet nurses had responded for military duty in much greater proportion than did their classmates who were not in the Corps ("The Cadet Nurse Corps," 1945).

Summary

The Corps promised to provide young women a lifetime education. Was this promise fulfilled? Let us consider the story of the young lady from Kansas described at the beginning of this chapter. Although her father's parting words, "Don't come home crying," made Donna Rae angry, she made up her mind to make the most of the program. If she didn't, she vowed that her mother and dad would never know. Donna Rae graduated from the Lincoln General Hospital School of Nursing and married a hometown boy who had returned from military service. She worked part-time helping her husband earn his degree in forest management and enjoyed caring for her family. After her husband's untimely death, she attended the University of Kansas and attained a baccalaureate degree in Family and Child Development, a master's degree in Family Economics, and added 50 more graduate hours to her record.

The Corps provided Donna Rae with the opportunity for the beginning of a lifetime education. She practiced nursing for approximately 35 years and considered her most worthy contribution to be that of role model and counselor for nursing students. Her greatest joy was having student nurses express appreciation for her help when they completed an associate degree nursing program and became registered nurses. Donna Rae received many nursing awards including a proclamation signed by a Kansas governor and one from the State of Kansas Legislature. St. Catherine Hospital named a scholarship in her name.

Donna's son, daughter, and four granddaughters are also part of her important accomplishments. Donna did not settle for choosing either homemaking or a career. She, like thousands of other women of her time, defied tradition and succeeded in both.

References

Advertising news and notes. (1944, January 6). New York Times, p. 28.

The cadet nurse corps. (1945). Journal of the American Medical Association, 127(15), 995.

Cadet nurse corps anniversary celebration. (1994, Summer). American Association for the History of Nursing Bulletin, p. 8

Henderson, J. (1945). One blueprint for recruitment. American Journal of Nursing, 45(12), 1002-1005.

Kalisch, B.J., & Kalisch, P.A. (1973). Cadet nurse with a future. Nursing Outlook, 21, 444-449.

Minnesota cadet nurse corps campaign. (1994). USOWI (Cadet Nurse File). Bethesda, MD: National Library of Medicine.

One good cadet recruits another. (1945, July). Cadet Nurse Corps News, 1, p. 3.

So proudly we hail! (1944, January). Scholastic, p. 12.

United States Office of War Information in Cooperation with the Division of Nurse Education (1945, May). Nurses are needed, the U.S. cadet nurse corps. (USPHS booklet from the Cadet Nurse File). Bethesda, MD: National Library of Medicine.

United States War Advertising Council in Cooperation with the Office of War Information and USPHS. (No date). How advertisers can cooperate with the U.S. cadet nurse corps. (Booklet from Cadet Nurse File). Bethesda, MD: National Library of Medicine.

Untitled news item. (1945, June). Cadet Nurse Corps News, 1. p. 4. (Cadet Nurse Corps File). Bethesda, MD: National Library of Medicine.

Wanted: Cadet nurses. (1944, June). Parents, p. 40.

War activities within the states. (1943). American Journal of Nursing, 43(9), 854.

5

The Maltese Cross Marches Again
by Thelma M. Robinson

According to Lucile Petry Leone, U.S. Cadet Nurse Corps emeritus chief nurse, one of the questions frequently asked was "Should cadet nurses have a uniform?" (L. P. Leone, personal communication, March 24, 1994). In planning for the Corps, a small survey was conducted. The responses showed cadet nurses needed an identity.

During World War II many opportunities were available for women to wear a uniform, showing their involvement in a wartime service. A uniform also had strong appeal for young women recruits. So it was decided the U.S. Cadet Nurse Corps would be a uniformed service.

In mid-July 1943, the *New York Times* announced that a cadet nurse would wear the uniform of her own school of nursing while on duty in the hospital, but each cadet would be provided an outdoor uniform that would identify her as a member of the Corps. The details of the design were not available at the time, although the uniform would be "pretty and feminine" rather than military ("100,000 Are Expected," 1943).

On August 16, 1943, the National Nursing Council for War Service sponsored a luncheon in New York City at the Waldorf Astoria Hotel to select the uniform for cadet nurses. Surgeon General Thomas Parran took time out from his busy schedule to attend the fashion show with other dignitaries ("Uniforms Chosen," 1943). Dr. Parran brought word from Paul V. McNutt, chair of the War Manpower Commission, who said the same priorities would be given to women in essential industries who wished to transfer to the United States Cadet Nurse Corps as given to recruits who joined the WACs, WAVES, SPARS, and Marine Corps Women's Reserve (U.S. Federal Security Agency/USPHS, 1950).

Frances P. Bolton, congressional representative and sponsor of the nursing training law, emphasized that the U.S. Cadet Nurse Corps was a necessary war measure and student nurses needed to feel a part of the great military strength of the country. Bolton (1943) congratulated the three designer finalists for their uniform models. She then told the jury of 32 fashion editors of national magazines, radio, and movies that the uniform to be selected should be style-right, business-like, and charming. The group selected the Molly Parnis wardrobe as the official street uniform to be worn with the Sally Victor beret. The well-known New York milliner designed the beret after one worn by General Montgomery ("Style Right Uniforms," 1943).

On September 5, 1943, Lucile Petry came to the White House wearing the striking gray uniform with red epaulets and jaunty Montgomery beret. Miss Petry's mission was to explain the work and purpose of the Corps to visiting Mrs. Winston Churchill and her daughter Mary. Miss Churchill wore the uniform of the British Auxiliary Territorial Service ("The Churchills," 1943).

The Corps had no military status, which caused difficulties in securing materials for the cadet nurse uniform under the priority controls of the War Production Board. The first enlistees of the Corps waited months for their uniforms. The New York Times reported in November 1943 that Montgomery berets would be popping up all over the American landscape soon after the first of the year ("Berets," 1943). At the time, it was hoped that uniform production would catch up by supplying the 88,491 members of the Cadet Nurse Corps with uniforms. It was late spring, however, before enrollees (95,000 in more than 1,000 schools of nursing) received their uniforms ("Gray and Scarlet Badge," 1945).

Petry models cadet nurse uniform for Mrs. Winston Churchill. On September 5, 1943, Director Lucile Petry (middle) came to the White House to model the new U.S. Cadet Nurse Corps uniform for visiting Mrs. Winston Churchill. Daughter Mary Churchill (right) was wearing the uniform of the British Auxiliary Territorial Service.

Margery Shanfelt Bitter, attending the University of Minnesota School of Nursing, wrote the following letter to her parents:

> You know the pictures of the cadet nurses in uniform on the posters? Well, I'm coming up in the world. Now I can say that my shoes have been worn with a uniform. They ... pulled out a couple of uniforms for two of the girls to have their pictures taken for the newspapers the other day and one of them borrowed my shoes! It makes me hopping mad to have them come out with one or two uniforms every time there's a public event and pictures to be taken. Then they snatch them back. The uniforms are beautiful, but I wish they could include a blouse (written 4/14/44).

Cadet nurses not only furnished their own blouses but shoes as well. With shoe rationing, questions were raised. On April 29, 1944, Corps Director Lucile Petry issued a memorandum, which indicated, "It is deemed advisable to urge the U.S. Cadet Nurses to use their own shoe ration coupon for the outdoor uniform shoes" (USPHS, 1944).

During World War II every individual was entitled to two pairs of wearable or repairable shoes. Director Petry informed cadets that if they had but one pair of wearable or repairable shoes it was possible for a cadet to obtain a special ration coupon from her local Office of Price Administration. All citizens were given the right to buy the shoes needed for ordinary wear by using the stamps in their ration books. Cadet nurses were reminded that they did not "need" extra shoes.

Cadet nurses who were enrolled in the Lincoln General Hospital School of Nursing remember the day their uniforms arrived. Sophie Teeters Nurses' Home in Lincoln, Nebraska, buzzed with excitement. They tried on their uniforms. Some did not fit well leaving wearers to speculate whether errors were made in measurement or the cadet gained or lost weight.

Donning the gray wool berets, the cadets tried to match the magazine model by draping the side. They formed a line in front of the one full-length mirror on the third floor of the dormitory to admire themselves in their uniforms.

Each cadet received a gray wool flannel winter suit and reefer coat with a half belt at the back waistline. The two summer suits were styled exactly as the winter suit but were made of gray and white striped cotton fabric. A gray raincoat completed the summer uniform. Red shoulder epaulets and silver buttons with the United States Public Health Service insignia enhanced the distinctive cadet nurse uniforms.

A gray fur felt beret with side drape could be worn with either the winter or summer uniform. This was allowed because some cadets never did receive a summer hat. Some cadets received a gray felt bowler hat with a red band but these were in short supply. The oval-shaped handbag with a shoulder strap was issued with an all-wool gray flannel cover for winter that could be changed to a white cover for the summer.

The cadets furnished their own blouses, shoes, scarves, and stockings. Decorated stockings were taboo as was leg makeup, brown-colored cosmetics applied to the legs—the wartime solution to the hosiery shortage (U.S. Federal Security Agency/ USPHS/Division of Nurse Education, 1945).

The red epaulet markings were plain for pre-cadets. Junior cadets wore one silver Maltese cross centered on each epaulet and senior cadets wore two. The oval sleeve patch with an eight-point Maltese cross was an early symbol of nursing, dating to the Knights Hospitalers of the First Crusade over 800 years ago ("Gray and Scarlet," 1945). Each of the eight points on the cross was meant to represent one of the beatitudes of the Sermon on the Mount. The Maltese cross as a whole symbolized human compassion and life-saving skills-an appropriate symbol for cadet nurses (U.S. Federal Registry, 1943).

In June 1944, General Montgomery was interviewed by a war correspondent and heard about a group of American girls wearing berets similar to his. The British commander requested details. Corps Director Petry dispatched a cable giving a complete description of the cadet nurse uniform and the services provided by the cadet nurses. She told the English general how becoming his beret was and suggested he recall the adage about imitation being the sincerest form of flattery. Recalling the incident years later, Director Petry said: "Cadet nurses modeling the general's beret was never a problem" ("Montgomery Learns About Cadet Nurses' Beret," 1944, p. 787).

The official U.S Cadet Nurse Corps rouge and lipstick, "Rocket Red" by Lentheric, matched the bright red trim on the gray uniform. The cosmetic company offered the makeup in gray plastic containers, with the Maltese cross motif in red. By November 1944 the rouge and lipstick sets were on sale at cosmetic counters in many cities ("Lipstick for Cadet Nurses," 1944).

The first issue of the *Cadet Nurse Corps News* (1945) announced a "snappy" new posture manual, *Figuratively Speaking*. This manual provided exercises for poor posture and showed cadet nurses how to wear the trim gray and scarlet uniform with all the "svelte and verve it deserved" ("Gray and Scarlet Badge of Distinction," 1945).

Dorothy Ford Larson recalled the day when the proud cadets at St. Luke's Hospital in Kansas City, Missouri, received their uniforms. They thought that the suits were wonderful but that the skirts were too long. The cadets hurriedly turned up the hems. Dorothy said, "I am always amused with the pictures of cadet nurses in uniform ... often showing inept hemming."

Cadet nurses took government regulations to heart in the wearing of the uniform. Margaret Smith Fairbanks, from Buffalo Hospital Sisters of Charity in Buffalo, New York, attended a theater in uniform with a tall classmate. A man in the row behind asked the tall cadet to remove her hat so he could see the movie. Margaret said, "My friend informed him that she was not allowed to remove her beret in public."

Each school of nursing designated special times when their cadet nurses were required to appear in uniform. Otherwise, wearing the uniform was optional. In the fall of 1946, the Ellis Hospital School of Nursing in Schenectady, New York, requested that student nurses wear their uniforms to attend a baccalaureate service in a downtown church. Mary Cooley Razewski and her friend Eileen Duval started early for the walk to the church. Along the way, two young men working for a General Electric-sponsored television show, *Ladies Be Seated*, stopped them. They were looking for participants in uniform and offered the young women $5 each to appear on the WGF television program. The cadet nurses accepted.

The next day a note appeared on the bulletin board stating that some students were conspicuous by being absent from the service; Mary's and Eileen's names were listed in the note. They reported to their principal and confessed what they had done. She informed the cadets that they were vain young ladies. The cadet nurses omitted the money part. "We didn't want our principal to think we were also greedy," Mary said.

Betty Deming Pearson, who attended the University of Minnesota School of Nursing, remembered a fund raising dinner event for the United Service Organizations (USO) for which cadet nurses had volunteered to serve as waitresses. Dean Katharine Densford was there wearing her summer gray and white striped cotton uniform. She came up to Betty Pearson and said,"My we tall women are elegant in our cadet nurse uniforms." Betty believed it was true.

Gertrude Sweet Adams recalled that when the uniforms finally arrived at State University School of Nursing in Plattsburg, New York, the cadets were ecstatic. Proud of her uniform, Gertrude wore it home the first weekend it was available. Unlike their peers in the military services, cadet nurses in most schools of nursing had little time to learn military protocols. When they first appeared in uniform in public, servicemen often saluted them and the cadets weren't sure what they should do. Cadet nurses soon learned that in their civilian status they should acknowledge a salute with a smile or a nod.

Dorothy Klingla Freeze attended the Los Angeles County General Hospital School of Nursing. The cadets there did not receive their uniforms until the middle of their second year.

She said, "We were so proud when our uniforms finally arrived. My favorite was the classy soft gray flannel winter uniform with the perky beret worn with white gloves and black pumps.

The USO canteens admitted only uniformed personnel and the cadets went there often. They found Earl Carroll's Hollywood Canteen a wonderful place to spend an evening seeing movie stars, dancing, and meeting people from all walks of life. "When the canteen became crowded we headed for the Palladium. Big name bands like Les Brown, Tommy Dorsey, and Stan Kenton played there. We danced till we dropped," reported Dorothy.

Virginia L. Wakefield Broom attended the Protestant Deaconess Hospital School of Nursing in Evansville, Indiana. She and other cadets served food and danced with servicemen at the USO on off-duty hours. She wore her cadet uniform because she had few other clothes. Broom said, "I felt proud to show the 'boys' that I too was helping win the war."

Dorothie Melvin Crowley's father, a newspaper photographer, took a picture of her in uniform, which was featured on the cover of the Valentine's Day Society section of the *Long Beach Press-Telegram*. The photograph showed Dorothie stepping out of a heart decorated with flowers and a lacy border. She said, "I felt like a movie star."

Another time her father took a picture of Dorothie and her girlfriend in their uniforms when they visited their old high school. Dorothie's former teacher in Home Arts invited then to talk to her class about nurses' training.

Another cadet, Anne Higgins Murphy, said:

I loved the Cadet Nurse Corps uniform and wore it on the New York Central Railroad when I went home because they gave us reduced rates, as did some of the New York City theaters and museums.

My best memory of wearing the uniform happened in June 1944 when my brother had his last visit home with the family before going to Europe. We had family pictures taken and I wore my cadet corps uniform. We looked happy! A few months later my brother was killed in action.

However not all cadet nurses loved their uniforms. Margery Truscott Barnett said, "Cadet uniform? How we hated them! We were required to wear them for many occasions and I despised those horrible shoes." Some schools required the wearing of sturdy Cuban-heel, laced oxfords, the regulation footwear for women in military service. However, because of war rationing and because the cadets paid for their own shoes, most were allowed to choose what shoes they would wear with their uniforms.

Some cadets wore their uniforms as infrequently as possible. Phyllis Brooks Theiss said, "We were issued cadet uniforms but I do not remember wearing mine. It was a waste of money for our group."

Representative Bolton (center) said, "We want our students to [believe they are] a part of the great military strength of this country." She is shown with cadets from the Frances Payne Bolton School of Nursing, Western Reserve University (now Case Western Reserve University) in Cleveland, Ohio, circa 1944.

Another group of cadets was disappointed when they learned they would never own uniforms. These were the young women who entered the Corps after World War II ended. Their disappointment was offset, however, by the knowledge that the Corps would accept applicants until October 15, 1945. This last class of cadets received all the Corps benefits and privileges—except the uniforms.

Millions of Americans between 1944 and 1948 acquired an image of nursing because of the uniform of the U.S. Cadet Nurse Corps. Most of us felt fortunate that we were issued a cadet uniform and admit that we enjoyed the sudden visibility. For one thing, wearing the uniform showed that we were doing our part in winning the war on the home front.

References

Berets to be worn by cadet nurses. (1943, November 23). The New York Times, p. 20.

Bolton, F.P. (1943, September). The U.S. cadet nurse corps. Hospital Progress, p. 272.

The Churchills admire American uniform. (1943, September 5). The New York Times, p. 19.

Gray and scarlet badge of distinction. (1945, June). Cadet Nurse Corps News, 1, pp. 2-4.

Lipstick for cadet nurses. (1944). American Journal of Nursing, 44(11), 1079.

Montgomery learns about cadet nurses' beret. (1944). American Journal of Nursing, 44(8), 787.

100,000 are expected to enroll in the new U.S. cadet corps. (1943, July 14). The New York Times, p. 14.

Style right uniforms assured U.S. cadet nurse corps. (1943, September). Hospital Progress, 273.

Uniforms chosen for cadet nurses. (1943, August, 17). The New York Times, p. 19.

United States Federal Security Agency. (1950). The U.S. cadet nurse corps 1943-1948. (PHS Publication No. 38, pp. 26, 30). Washington, DC: United States Government Printing Office.

United States Federal Registry. (1943, July 9). Part 30. Uniform and insignia of the United States cadet nurse corps. (Title 42-Public Health, Chapter 1). Washington,DC: USPHS, Federal Security Agency.

United States Federal Security Agency, USPHS, Division of Nurse Education (1945, November). U.S. cadet nurse uniforms. USPHS Bulletin. (RG 90). Washington, DC: National Archives and Records Administration.

USPHS. (1944, April 29). Cadet nurse shoe rationing policy. (Memorandum to Professional Staff from Lucile Petry). (RG 90). Washington, DC: National Archives and Records Administration.

6

Cadet Nurse in Review
by Thelma M. Robinson

Cadence count! Coll-yum march! Eyes right!

In preparation for the first nationwide induction ceremony, cadet nurses throughout the country practiced military drill. Corps Director Lucile Petry stood in review of cadet nurses on the Georgetown University campus drill field. Officers of the 703rd Military Police Battalion trained the female "rookies" and expressed confidence that the cadet nurses would present a trim and smart appearance in their gray and red uniforms. Surgeon General Thomas Parran said:

> Although the U.S. Cadet Nurse Corps is not a military organization, knowledge of military carriage and the significance of wearing a uniform with pride and distinction will be a valuable asset to its members. By improving posture, so important to a nurse who must be on her feet many hours of the day, this military drill should help cadet nurses in their work (Division of Nurse Education, 1945).

The surgeon general had an even better reason for encouraging cadet nurses to don their uniforms and march; the ranks of missing nurses on the home front had to be filled and parading cadet nurses enhanced the recruitment effort.

On May 13, 1944, nationwide induction ceremonies conducted officially and simultaneously brought 96,000 student nurses from more than 1,000 schools of nursing into the Corps. The keynote induction ceremony with 750 cadet nurses representing nine local schools of nursing took place in

Washington, D.C. Held in the Daughters of the American Revolution (DAR) Constitution Hall, this ceremony was broadcast over the NBC network with 250 radio station hookups throughout the country. From New York to California and North Dakota to Texas, cadet nurses assembled in groups, listening and waiting to repeat the Cadet Nurse Pledge led by a local dignitary.

In New York City a color guard from the Army post at Fort Jay headed the procession as 1,300 cadet nurses marched into the City Hall Plaza to the music of the Department of Sanitation Band. Some cadets wore the smart gray uniform of the Corps while others wore their student nurse uniforms.

Mayor LaGuardia warned the cadets that nursing was hard work. He told them he had just recovered from being sick and he wouldn't want to be the nurse who cared for him. Throughout New York City, 2,446 other cadets on duty in 47 hospitals found a radio and paused in their work. When the time came, they joined in repeating the Cadet Nurse Pledge led by Mayor LaGuardia ("1,300 Cadet Nurses," 1944).

At the Washington, D.C., induction a cadet nurse described how she felt when she entered Constitution Hall in the opening processional:

> I had a deep feeling of thankfulness and pride in my chosen profession. On the stage 48 cadet nurses stood before the flags of the different states. A cadet nurse guarded the impressive flag of the surgeon general of the U.S. Public Health Service-blue with the caduceus and anchor-and another stood watch over the new banner of the Corps; [it had] a gray field with silver Maltese cross blazing in a center of red. After we were seated, Captain Burgess Meredith, USAAF, more familiar to us as a motion picture star, described the beautiful scene. The huge flag of the United States rippled down from the ceiling and came to rest far above our heads ["National Induction," 1944, pp. 592-593].

First Lady Eleanor Roosevelt told how she had witnessed nurses serving on the battlefields of the world and commended the cadets' work on the home front. Bing Crosby, via Hollywood, sang a song dedicated to the cadets. Helen Hayes' stirring reading, "Remember Tomorrow," portrayed the gift cadet nurses were giving to their country. Congresswoman Frances P. Bolton explained to the audience that the Corps would assure a continuous flow of graduate nurses pledged to essential nursing for the duration of the war. Corps Director Lucile Petry told the cadets they were carrying on a tradition, which represented the finest of American womanhood.

Now it came time for cadet nurses to give their pledge. Across America, cadets stood at attention. In Washington, D.C., Surgeon General Parran reminded cadets this was a great moment in their lives, one that would be treasured for years to come. He also said that it was a great moment for him as chief of Public Health Service to administer the Cadet Nurse Pledge for the cadets in our nation's capital.

In Madison, Wisconsin, four schools of nursing came together in the Madison General Hospital School of Nursing auditorium. Cadet Nurse Edith Tullis Olsen remembered Governor Goodland leading her group in reciting the Cadet Nurse Corps Pledge.

I was in Lincoln Nebraska.

> I joined 100 cadet nurses at St. Paul Methodist Church for the Cadet Nurse Induction Ceremony. Hazel Hinds, director of our school of nursing and the former chair of the Red Cross Recruitment Committee for military nurses, introduced Chief Justice of Nebraska, Robert G. Simmons. When he asked us to stand, the rustle of our starched aprons brought smiles to attending guests. We wore our hospital uniforms with the Maltese patch on our sleeves. Our cadet nurse uniforms had not arrived.

Cadet nurses linked by radio came together from across America. Together we recited our pledge:

> I am solemnly aware of the obligations I assume toward my country and my chosen profession; I shall follow faithfully the instructions and guidance of my instructors and the physicians with whom I shall work; I shall keep my body strong and my mind alert, and my heart steadfast; I shall be kind, tolerant, and understanding. Above all, I will dedicate myself now and forever to the triumph of life

Six hundred cadet nurses from 12 hospitals in Greater Kansas City, Missouri, raised white-gloved right hands for the Cadet Nurse Pledge in the Kansas City Municipal auditorium on May 12, 1945. Dr. Thomas Parran, surgeon general of the U.S. Public Health Service, led the pledge over a national radio hookup from New York City, climaxing the second annual national induction program.

over death. As a cadet nurse, I pledge to my country my service in essential nursing for the duration of the war.

A year later on May 12, 1945, more than 1,100 schools of nursing throughout the 48 states, District of Columbia, and Puerto Rico observed the second annual national induction of Cadet Nurse Corps members. Many schools of nursing again organized citywide induction programs. Cadets unable to attend were asked to pause briefly in their hospital duties to renew their pledge and rededicate their service to military or essential civilian nursing for the duration of the war (Division of Nurse Education, 1945).

Helen Lewis Gustin from the Nebraska Methodist Hospital School of Nursing took part in this event with a group of 283 student nurses in Omaha. By this time the cadets had received their uniforms. Gustin said, "We were inducted into the Cadet

Nurse Corps wearing our uniforms, some in the summer [version] and some in the winter version. Our 60-voice Cadet Nurse Corps choir opened the ceremony."

A previous public relations officer for General Patton's Third Army, Major P. D. Widiner from Camp Carson, Colorado, spoke at the event. And while the event was taking place, some senior cadet nurses from Nebraska along with other cadets were stationed at Camp Carson caring for servicemen who had returned from the Battle of the Bulge and were recovering from frozen hands and feet (Fagan, 1992).

In Washington, D.C., for the second induction ceremony, representatives of radio and stage paid tribute to the Corps. Edgar Bergen and Charlie McCarthy told cadet nurse Rosemary Valdez that they "couldn't resist the girls in gray and scarlet." Dr. Thomas Parran from a New York broadcasting studio led the pledge that brought an additional 112,000 student nurses nationwide into the Corps ("A Souvenir," 1945).

Once the novelty of being in uniform was over, cadet nurses needed to address other issues. One was that they did not march well. Petronella Buck Arledge said:

> We didn't know the first thing about marching. I was at Hillcrest Memorial Hospital School of Nursing in Waco, Texas, where administrators tried to remedy the situation. Drill sergeants were called out from the local military bases to teach the cadet nurses to march correctly.

> The drill sergeant told us to pick up a rock and carry it in our right hand, but we still had a hard time telling our right foot from the left.

Alberta Wallace Beddo, another cadet nurse from Hillcrest, remembered the following:

> The language ... and the impatience of the sergeants scared us. Our group, however, turned out to be a striking addition to military parades, even though we weren't always in step. Our lovely

uniforms and smiles of pride made up for our marching inadequacies.

Virginia Bogan Charnock said:

We marched to our classes at Canisius College at Buffalo, New York, and returned marching. We wanted to show off our uniforms to the all-male Air Cadets, who were in uniform and marched to their classes as well. We sang while we marched.

The military required women to wear sturdy regulation footwear. But cadet nurses paid for their own shoes and usually wore stylish shoes such as pumps. Some cadets admitted their feet ached after a parade that took them down brick streets.

Cadets sang and marched to the tune of the U.S. Cadet Nurse Corps March. Edmund Ziman wrote the music. The lyrics that follow were by Beatrice Ziman:

The Maltese cross is marching again to answer the call.
A new crusade we give our care to valorous men
To heroes and all who need our aid.
We're the cadets, we're in the Corps
Doing our part to help the nation win the war,
Doing the job we're chosen for
United States Cadet Nurse Corps.
(Ziman & Ziman, 1944).

Wearing the cadet uniform provided some interesting advantages. Rosemary Hanson Seals from the St. Louis City Hospital School of Nursing tells of one such advantage:

We went to the Methodist Church on Sundays and those in uniform always received an invitation for Sunday dinner. This gave the cadets an opportunity to meet soldiers and sailors. People often stopped us on the street and asked us what country we were from. Few people knew about the Cadet Nurse Corps.

One poignant memory will never be forgotten. A fellow cadet nurse became ill and died from an infection.

Rosemary Seals and another classmate served as "honor guards" during the viewing and at the funeral. They stood at attention in cadet nurse uniforms at both ends of the casket.

On a happier occasion, Dorothie Melvin Crowley served with the color guard along with nurses from the Army and Navy at the Hollywood Bowl Sunrise Service.

> We were thrilled to be on stage in front of thousands of people in the audience. A beautiful 12-year-old girl who later became a movie star sang a solo on that early Easter morning. Along with us, she waited nervously backstage with her mother. After the event we took armloads of Easter lilies back to Los Angeles County General Hospital.

In keeping with the patriotic spirit, Dr. H. Sargent, a veteran of World War I, initiated a flag raising ceremony at Milwaukee County General Hospital. Cadet nurses purchased a bugle and took turns heralding the day promptly at 6:30 a.m. Flag bearers in cadet or hospital uniforms were selected each day from the ranks of the older students. At sundown, taps sounded as the flag was lowered ("Sunrise Ceremony," 1945).

The USPHS encouraged esprit de corps and seized every opportunity to attract publicity for the cadets. On the first anniversary, July 1, 1944, Surgeon General Parran presented the white, silver, and scarlet U.S. Cadet Nurse Corps flag emblazoned with the Maltese cross to Corps Director Petry on the steps of the Public Health Service building on Constitution Avenue in Washington, D.C. The surgeon general said:

> We know what these banners mean to the men who fight and die for them. We look to them as our symbol of united strength, loyalty, honor, and heroic sacrifice. What is a more fitting tribute to a vital and patriotic organization than that its first "battle flag" be added to those now flying in the vanguard of the Allied cause. ("The Cadet Corps," 1944, p. 786).

The official flag of the U.S. Cadet Nurse Corps featuring the symbol of the Maltese cross is proudly displayed by two cadets.

Director Lucile Petry accepted the banner on behalf of the Corps and said that the flag represented the desire of every cadet nurse to be of service to her country.

A year later on July 1, 1945, the Cadet Nurse Corps News published information about the second anniversary:

> Like [it has] their brothers, the trust of responsibility has matured them-made them invaluable citizens of a world at war.... Because they have learned to care for the nation's sick, many now shoulder the burden of caring for the nation's wounded.... The nation looks to them for leadership. Although their average age is only 19, cadet nurses have a splendid record of achievement. They have released graduate nurses for military service. They have maintained essential nursing service in civilian hospitals. ("Birthday Remembrances," 1945, p. 1).

The second anniversary was on a Sunday and many cadets went to church. Many from Freedmen's Hospital School of Nursing in Washington, D.C., attended the Third Baptist Church. Founded in 1894, Freedmen's was one of America's oldest and largest schools of nursing for black women. The pastor called upon the cadets to sing the Corps' new hymn:

> Faithful ever to my country,
> To the Corps, my sacred trust.
> Grant that I may follow wisely,
> All the guidance offered me.
> Give me kindness, Grant me patience
> That I may not fail this noble challenge.
> Here to heal the suffering ones
> ("New Hymn is Special," 1945).

R. Dean Shure, composer of church music and director of music at the Mt. Vernon Methodist Church in Washington, D.C., wrote the music. A member of the staff of the Division of Nurse Education wrote the words for the Cadet Nurse Corps Hymn.

Several other events honoring the Cadet Nurse Corps' second anniversary occurred. Following is a list of some of those events.

- In Independence, Missouri, President Truman reviewed plans for the Corps for the coming year and Mrs. Truman cut the Corps' cake at the Independence Sanitarium ("Cadet Nurse Corps Celebrates," 1945).
- In Wichita, Kansas, the second anniversary of the first production-model B-29 flight coincided with that of the Cadet Nurse Corps. A B-29 was christened and named for the Corps.
- In New York City a group of 600 uniformed cadets gathered in Times Square to participate in a birthday war-bond rally. Cadet nurses scurried to and fro selling slices of the "largest birthday cake in the world" in the war bond effort ("Birthday Remembrances," 1945, p.3).
- In Philadelphia cadets were honored at the "Army Nurse

in War"exhibit when the baker's union contributed a 3-foot high cake. Speakers included Katharine J. Densford, president of the American Nurses Association, and Captain Mary Haggerty of the Army Nurse Corps.

- In Boston more than 5,000 people attended the second anniversary celebration of the Cadet Nurse Corps. Governor Tobin took part, along with Corps Director Petry, Benny Goodman, and Helen Hayes. Beatrice Graham Whitney, a graduate of Massachusetts Memorial Hospital School of Nursing in Boston, was given the Avon Award as the typical cadet nurse of America.

The war had been won when the nation's health leaders congratulated the Cadet Nurse Corps on their third birthday in 1946. The July 1946 issue of the *Cadet Nurse Corps News* reported that cadet nurses had a glorious record of achievement during the war years. Peter D. Ward, MD, and president of the American Hospital Association thanked the cadets for a job well done. He said, "Now, even though the fighting is over, the need for nurses is still great, and Corps members and graduates will continue to be a credit to their country as they enter upon a professional career bright with opportunity ("Health Leaders Congratulate," 1946).

Roger I. Lee, MD, president of the American Medical Association, said, "You have chosen a distinguished career; one which will bring you self-satisfaction gained from helping your fellow man. In peace, as in war, this is a noble achievement ("Health Leaders Congratulate," 1946).

Nurse leader Katharine J. Densford congratulated "the cadet nurse of today ... the graduate professional nurse of tomorrow!" She also told the cadets, "The future holds rich promises. Go forward to meet it with confidence and with hope."

To cadet nurses everywhere, Surgeon General Thomas Parran sent a congratulatory message through the *Cadet Nurse Corps News* on the Corps' fourth birthday, July 1, 1947:

Although our country has successfully made the transition from war to peace, demands for nursing service are increasing steadily, while new opportunities are opening up on every hand. To the graduates, and soon-to-be graduates of the Cadet Nurse Corps, I extend birthday greetings and best wishes for success in your professional careers ("Cadet Nurse Corps is Four," 1947).

No fanfare greeted the Corps on its fifth birthday. The last issue of the *Cadet Nurse Corps News* had been printed in January and the phase-out date of October 15, 1948, was fast approaching. Cadet Paulie Morey [Perry] along with other senior cadets, were completing their studies and work in assigned civilian and federal hospitals and other health organizations.

Summary

Standing in review, marching in parades, selling war bonds, and attending church in uniform were all new experiences that gave cadet nurses confidence and pride. Our nation's leaders had summoned them, teenage girls of World War II, with a challenge to resolve the country's critical nurse shortage. They came forth to serve. What an honor! What a privilege! What an opportunity!

References

Birthday remembrances for the cadet nurse scrapbook. (1945, September). **Cadet Nurse News,** 1, p.3. (Cadet Nurse File). Bethesda, MD: National Library of Medicine.

The cadet corps' first birthday. (1944). American Journal of Nursing, 44(8), p. 786.

Cadet nurse corps is four years old July 1. (1947, July). **Cadet Nurse Corps News,** 2, p. 1. (Cadet Nurse File). Bethesda, MD: National Library of Medicine.

Cadet nurse corps celebrates second birthday. (1945). **American Journal of Nursing,** 45(6), 656-657.

Division of Nurse Education, USPHS. (1945, May 7). **News release (through Office of War Information) to morning newspapers.** [RG 90]. Washington, DC: National Archives and Records Administration.

Fagan, M.L. (1992). **Nebraska History,** p. 133.

Health leaders congratulate corps on birthday. (1946, July). **Cadet Nurse Corps News,** 1, p. 3. (Cadet Nurse File). Bethesda, MD: National Library of Medicine.

National induction as seen by a cadet nurse. (1944). **American Journal of Nursing,** 44(6), 592-593.

New hymn is special corps birthday gift. (1945, July). **Cadet Nurse Corps News,** 1, p. 2. (Cadet Nurse File). Bethesda, MD: National Library of Medicine.

1,300 cadet nurses are inducted by mayor in city hall plaza. (1944, May 14). **The New York Times,** p. 26.

A souvenir of your 1945 induction. (1945, July). **Cadet Nurse Corps News,** 1, pp. 1-2. (Cadet Nurse File). Bethesda, MD: National Library of Medicine.

Sunrise ceremony. (1945, November). Cadet Nurse Corps News, 1. (Cadet Nurse File). Bethesda, MD: National Library of Medicine.

United States Division of Nurse Education, Federal Security Agency, USPHS. (1944, April 29). U.S. cadet nurse corps military drill. (News release to Washington, D.C., newspapers). [RG 90]. Washington, DC: National Archives and Records Administration.

Ziman, E., & Ziman, B. (1944). **U.S. cadet nurse corps march.** (RG 90). Washington, DC: National Archives and Records Administration.

7

GIVE ME 5 MINUTES MORE: THE PRE-CADET
by Paulie M. Perry

As a probie and pre-cadet I mopped floors during lunch hours and washed windows during hospital visiting hours (Grace Dannenberg)

Arnot-Ogden Memorial Hospital in Elmira, New York, did not have enough housekeeping staff and had only one orderly for the entire hospital. Mopping floors didn't bother Grace Rohde Dannenberg until the following incident occurred. A new patient called, "Nurse!" She went over to him and asked how she could help. He opened his eyes, glanced at her and said, "I'm sorry, I thought you were a nurse." "I couldn't blame him [because] as a probie I wore no cap and he had seen me mopping the floor when he was admitted." However, Grace progressed from menial tasks to learning to give nursing care. When she gave personal care to patients she "enjoyed being a probie the most!"

Nursing students in hospital schools of nursing had a probation period that varied in length among schools. Because they were on probation, students received the nickname of "probies." Their curricula included introduction to nursing arts theory and the practice of nursing procedures. Probies were scrutinized for grades and appearance; both had to be satisfactory for them to remain in school.

Preclinical cadets in university or college programs spent the first quarter or semester on campus and their grades determined if they would continue in the nursing program. Their schedules included scholastic instruction with no hospital ward experience. Hence the pre-cadets in university or college programs did not usually perform the same kind of duties as did those in most hospital schools of nursing.

Whether they answered to the name of probie or preclinical student, the women who joined the Corps were pre-cadets for the first 9 months and their future as nurses depended upon their achievements during this time. Those who did not measure up to the goals set by the school were dismissed. During this period pre-cadets welcomed the monthly stipend of $15 and eagerly awaited payday.

As pre-cadets at Lincoln General Hospital School of Nursing in Nebraska, my classmates and I started classes the day after we arrived at the nurses' residence. We quickly learned that study period was not optional but obligatory, enforced by the housemother who checked to see that we were in our rooms at 8:00 p.m. The pre-cadet course of study included: anatomy and physiology, chemistry, microbiology, drugs and solutions, nursing arts, personal hygiene, history of nursing, professional adjustments, and physical education (U.S. Federal Security Agency/ USPHS, 1950). Lincoln General Hospital School of Nursing had a contract with the University of Nebraska for the instruction of the science courses.

We 48 probies congregated at the corner bus stop by the nurses' residence to wait and crowd into the bus that took us to the university campus. Our chaperone, a diminutive lady with white hair wearing hat and gloves, gave each of us a nickel for the fare and accompanied us to our classes. She dozed during the lectures, lulled to sleep by the subject matter of the instructors.

The pre-cadets at the University of Minnesota School of Nursing received their academic studies on campus. University officials then divided the cadets among three hospitals for their practical nursing experience: University of Minnesota Hospital, Minneapolis General Hospital, Charles T. Miller Hospital.

Albina Borho Reichmuth remembered the experience like this:

We carried 20 credit hours of coursework for the first 3 months and had to maintain a C average. Three hundred out of 500 cadets made the first cut in my class. Pre-cadet students who passed the preclinical period went by [trolley] from the Minneapolis General Hospital dormitory to the campus for classes then returned for hospital duty. Often the trolley would be caught in rush-hour traffic and we would be late to go on duty.

Pre-cadets worked split shifts: 7 to 10 a.m. on the unit, off to class at the university, back to the hospital for duty from 7 to 10 p.m., then to the dorm to study. It wasn't easy. Many nights we studied until 2 a.m.

On the brighter side, the hospital had a carnival every year with the physicians, interns, residents, and nurses putting on a talent show. Also, pre-cadets could attend all university functions, such as ballets, symphonies, plays, and dances, as well as football and basketball games. Albina was on the softball and basketball teams, which competed with other hospital teams.

Aune Hautamaki Trygg recalled attending classes in the nursing arts laboratory at the University of Minnesota and giving practice saline injections into oranges before testing her skills on her classmates. Pre-cadets also practiced nursing procedures on Mrs. Chase, the life-sized mannequin who served as a willing, non-complaining, and silent patient.

Ruth Ericson Benson, also a pre-cadet at Minnesota, had these memories:

Reading a thermometer was my downfall. I couldn't seem to get it at the proper angle to see both the mercury and the graded scale on the thermometer. Shaking down the thermometer required quick flips of the wrist and if you stood too close to the bedside stand and accidentally broke the thermometer there was a price to pay. Careless probies who exceeded the breakage fee allowed by the university had to divvy up.

In November 1943 Surgeon General Parran sent his special commendation to the University of Minnesota School of Nursing for their tremendous response to the national nurse shortage emergency. The occasion was the Minnesota-Iowa football game. At half time University President Coffee stepped to the microphone and thanked Miss Densford, dean of the School of Nursing, whose leadership resulted in 1,125 cadet nurses being trained at the university. To the stadium and radio audience, President Coffee read Dr. Parran's telegram:

> Congratulations to the School of Nursing at the University of Minnesota for the magnificent effort it is making towards winning the war. You have enrolled in the United States Cadet Nurse Corps the largest number of students of any institution in the country. To make this possible you have greatly expanded teaching and housing facilities. The cadet nurses at Minnesota through their pledge to do military and civilian nursing are engaged in essential war service. My grateful appreciation to you, your faculty and students for your outstanding contribution (Gray, 1960, pp. 144-148).

Mildred Toney Johnstone of the St. Joseph School of Nursing in Orange, California, suffered homesickness for her family on a cattle ranch in northeast California, 800 miles away.

> I didn't get home for 14 months but made many friends because we were in the same age range, took the same subjects, and had the same goals and regulations. I studied hard as I did not want to fail. I promised myself I would never milk another cow.

> Although all the pre-cadets were required to go to choir, after 2 weeks I was excused because I could not carry a tune. Instead I went to the study hall. Perhaps this is why I finished at the top of my class.

Sometimes the many hours of studying backfired. Pre-cadet Janet Cruickshank Lippold of the Colorado Training School for Nurses in Denver, Colorado, was given an F on the microbiology quiz that tested pre-cadets on their knowledge of antitoxins and antibodies. The instructor wrote, "It is obvious you have studied hard because you were consistently wrong."

Phyllis Maxine MacGruder Deis of Miami Valley Hospital School of Nursing in Dayton, Ohio, had a different kind of challenge. "When trying to take the rectal temperature of a 24-year-old male, I couldn't seem to find the right spot for insertion. My instructor Miss Gerdes ushered me out into the hall and said 'Open your eyes and look!'" ("Nurses' Memories," 1996).

The motto of pre-cadets at Columbus Hospital School of Nursing in Milwaukee, Wisconsin, was, "Ours is not to question why; ours is but to do or die." Mary Janson St. Peter felt pushed to the maximum the day she was assigned nine bed baths to complete between 7:00 and 9:30 a.m. It did not go well. "However, the patients were wonderful and those who were able got out of bed to lend a hand. Some even answered signal lights," reported Mary.

Pre-cadets coped as best they could. The commute from Columbia Hospital to downtown Milwaukee Vocational School involved a 15-minute bus ride so Mary often took advantage of the travel time to take a nap. Another coping mechanism was climbing out the first floor window after the housemother's 10:00 p.m. bedtime to meet interns at Tony's for refreshments. On the return trip the policeman walking the beat in the neighborhood gave them a boost back through the window. "We were nearly caught," said Mary. At one point Mary and a friend got so discouraged they tried to enlist in the Coast Guard. "When they found out we were cadet nurses they showed us the door," recalled Mary.

Fatigue? Pre-cadets knew it well. If probies had 15 minutes between classes, they set their alarms and took a quick nap. When the alarm jolted them to semi-consciousness, they moaned, "Give Me Five Minutes More," the title of a hit song of the day.

Penicillin, the wonder drug of that time, had come into general use in the mid-40s. Nurses administered this new medication to patients intramuscularly every 3 hours around the clock. Cadet Maurine Kunkee Leonard felt honored to be the nurse chosen to give the first penicillin injection at Lincoln General Hospital.

Maurine carefully mixed the powdered penicillin with sterile water. The instructor watched as she drew up the penicillin into the syringe, warning her the patient could die if he had a reaction. "To make matters worse the patient lived in David City, Nebraska, my home town and his wife knew my family. I was a nervous wreck but all survived: patient, wife, supervisor, and I," said Maurine.

As a pre-cadet at the University of Minnesota, Patricia Ruby Morse learned how to prepare narcotics for hypodermic injection. She explained:

> Prior to giving a "hypo" I mixed the narcotic tablet with water then heated the solution in a spoon over a Bunsen burner sufficiently to dissolve the medication. I drew the proper dosage of solution into the syringe, stuck the needle into an alcohol-soaked cotton ball, and placed the syringe on a tray with the patient's medicine card to carry to the bedside for administration.
>
> We tested the needles for burrs and sharpened them as needed. Then we sterilized the needles and syringes between uses. I made sure the glass syringe barrel and plunger had the same numbers so they would fit correctly.

"As a probie I enjoyed the Nursing Arts class the most," Thelma Morey Robinson remembered. "I loved caring for patients with the nursing skills I was qualified to give at the time." In a letter to her mother she wrote:

> Today I volunteered to serve as a patient for a footbath and have now learned the requirements for over two hundred nursing procedures. We completed our class on printing, and are expected to chart legibly. I passed the test—printing the Florence Nightingale Pledge.

Robinson's nursing arts instructor became her role model and inspiration. Mrs. Sorrell showed how to give the healing touch and enlivened her lectures with humorous hospital stories. "The important first step of every procedure, 'Allay the patient's fear' (through patient education) has stuck with me all these 50 years of nursing practice," Thelma said.

Coming from a farm in Texas, Mary Tamplen Rupel was most fearful as a pre-cadet of getting lost in the large and forbidding Lubbock General Hospital.

> We had to learn so many facts and I lacked self-confidence. So I picked out the tallest and most confident girl, Sue, in my class. Sue lived in Lubbock before becoming a cadet and knew where to go. I followed Sue. This worked well until I gained self-reliance and learned my way around.

Stranger than rules were the protocols regarding relationships, never written, but profoundly understood. Shirley Morrison Francisco of the Meadville Hospital School of Nursing in Pennsylvania asked, "Was there a form of life lower than a probie student nurse? We probies were not allowed to enter the front door of the hospital."

When a physician appeared, student nurses jumped to their feet. Clinical instructors inspected bedside stands and beds to ensure all items were in their prescribed position. Bed linen corners were mitered and redone until nurse instructors approved. Striped bedspreads had to show the same number of stripes down each side. "We were called back on duty to rectify the slightest error. Sitting with a patient just to talk was strongly discouraged. To keep out of trouble, we cleaned, cleaned, cleaned, and cleaned," Shirley said.

Corinne Hallonquist Anderson said:

> Everything stopped until the doctor was accommodated, whether in the chart room or with a patient. Once when I was a pre-cadet at Emory University Hospital School of Nursing in Atlanta, Georgia, I was giving a patient a bed bath when a man carrying a black bag entered the room.
>
> I presumed he was the doctor and left the room. I did not know he was the barber who came to give shaves and haircuts. Of course this put me behind in my schedule of caring for my assigned patients before hurrying to class.

Living in the nurses' residence challenged Dolores Gast Struewing during her probie year. Some of the junior and senior students at Mercy Hospital School of Nursing in Hamilton, Ohio, made life miserable for new probies. "They sent us to the back of the line for bathroom privileges, stopped us in hallways to recite procedures, and demanded we carry notes from room to room, sew on buttons, or shine shoes," remembered Dolores. They also sent gullible probies to surgery or central supply for fallopian tubes. "Despite the demands and harassment, we developed many friendships that lasted through the years," Dolores said.

The probation period at West Texas School of Nursing in Lubbock proved valuable to Nadine Wilson Weeks. "I observed the junior and senior cadets for skills and knowledge and this helped me become a good nurse."

Pre-cadets learned the importance of a sense of humor. They took it in stride when they returned to their rooms and found mattresses upended or hanging out the window, or their beds short sheeted, thanks to upper classmates. Probies soon learned the trick of short sheeting-a special way of putting on the top sheet, making it impossible to get between the top and bottom sheets.

A pre-cadet from the South recalled a prank pulled on her class when they began the probation period. During the night the older cadets sneaked into the rooms of the pre-cadets and gathered up all their newly issued black duty shoes, identical except for size. When the pre-cadets awoke they found 28 pairs of black shoes, all mixed up, in the bathtub. Twenty-eight pre-cadets frantically sorted through the pile for a matched pair of shoes so they could be on duty before 7:00 a.m.

Faye Clark Berzon of Beth Israel Hospital School of Nursing in Boston spent much pre-cadet time in classes before being assigned patients on the hospital wards. Her first assignment was to prepare a dead body to be brought to the morgue. The procedure in the nursing arts text described the 26 steps, which included:

> In the hospital the removal of the body from the ward to the morgue should be conducted inconspicuously and with respect and dignity. Spare the other patients on the ward the details of the death, aftercare, and removal of the body (Harmer & Henderson, 1942, pp. 415-417).

"Why I did not quit after that, I don't know, but I didn't want to give up a free education or admit I couldn't take it, so I stayed," said Faye.

Beth Israel Hospital depended on student nurses for its primary staff, with junior and senior cadets as charge nurses. "As pre-cadets we resented taking orders from older students," Faye recalled, "but we followed the rules." Faye survived the pre-cadet trials and tribulations to receive the reward of being capped by the director of nursing. "The Cadet Nurse Corps gave me the beginning of my career in professional nursing," Faye said.

Pre-cadets soon learned the poignancy of birth, death, and pain. Ruby Hudgins Johns of Akron City Hospital School of Nursing in Ohio remembered:

> I found it easy to make beds with tight, smooth sheets and mitered corners, and to change sheets with the patient in the bed. As a pre-cadet at Akron City Hospital School of Nursing, I considered it fun to anticipate a patient's needs. The hard part was dealing with what I saw and heard from patients who were in pain and [still] being objective enough to perform well. Sometimes I wondered if I was cut out to be a nurse, so I went to the director of nurses and told her what I was feeling. The director listened and then told me it would get better as time went on. She also promised to do all she could to help me overcome my problem and she did on several occasions.

Pre-cadets shared the same frustrations regardless of the school of nursing. We studied and worked hard, complained and laughed together as we dreamed of the day when we would advance to junior cadet. Our youthful resiliency carried us through the tough times and took us closer to our first milestone—that of earning our caps—on our journey to becoming a nurse.

References

Nurses' memories. **Dayton Daily News.** (1996, May 3). P. C1, Dayton Ohio.

Gray, J. (1960). **Education for nursing: A history of the University of Minnesota school of nursing** (pp. 144-148). Minneapolis, MN: University of Minnesota Press.

Harmer, B., & Henderson, V. (1942). **The principles and practice of nursing** (pp. 415-417). New York: Macmillan.

United States Federal Security Agency. (1950). **The U.S. cadet nurse corps 1943-1948.** (PHS publication No. 38, pp. 36, 90). Washington, DC: United States Government Printing Office.

8

RITUALS, REWARDS, AND ROMPS
by Paulie M. Perry

The long awaited yet dreaded day arrived. Seated outside the director of nurses' office, I waited at the appointed hour to find out if I would get my student-nurse cap. If I achieved this, I could continue in the U.S. Cadet Nurse Corps and become a junior cadet in 3 months.

My heart pounded as I waited with freshly whitened shoes and hair pulled up in a net above my collar. The cadet nurse patch with the Maltese cross had been sewn on my left sleeve. Nervously I smoothed my white starched apron covering the blue and white striped hospital student uniform. The door opened and a classmate flew past. I tried to read her face. Was she happy? Sad? Angry?

In the inner sanctum of her office, the director chatted about my grades and gave me words of inspiration. After what seemed an eternity of suspense, she said, "Congratulations, Miss Morey, you passed your probation period." I rejoiced that I would participate in my school's traditional capping ceremony.

Rituals and Rewards

At "capping" ceremonies the presentation of a cap, unique to each school, concluded the probation period in hospital schools of nursing, and the preclinical period in collegiate and university nursing schools for pre-cadets across the nation. The details of this ritual varied. Each institution incorporated its unique and specific customs into its "rites of passage" ceremony for student nurses.

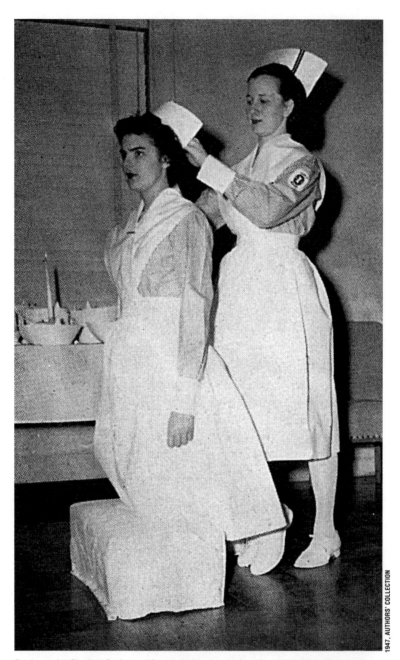

Senior cadet Claribel Carlson of Cozad, Nebraska, in the role of "big sister" pinned a cap on Barbara Bredenkamp of McCool Junction, Nebraska, at the Lincoln General Hospital School of Nursing capping ceremony. Cadets often received junior or senior stripes for their caps at the same capping ceremonies.

Rituals played an important part in the regimented schedule of student nurses during the first half of the 20th century. Schools of nursing required strict adherence to their rules; dismissal was the consequence for failure to submit to authority.

As recompense for obedience to this rigid control, schools of nursing provided rewards along the way, the first achievement occurring at the auspicious capping ceremony. Other enticements often included changing the student uniform by adding a bib to the apron, deleting the collar or tie from the dress, presenting stripes for student caps at junior or senior cadet levels, or progressing from black to white shoes and stockings.

Not all students were rewarded, however. Students who were found to be unsatisfactory were dismissed before the capping ceremony and in some instances as many as 1/3 of the class was dismissed.

At Lincoln General Hospital School of Nursing several classmates quietly packed their bags and departed for home. The rest of the class had 5 days in which to invite family and friends to their capping ceremony and to make final preparations for the big day.

Together pre-cadets recited the Florence Nightingale Pledge over and over so they would do it correctly at the capping ceremony.

> I solemnly pledge myself before God and in the presence of this assembly to pass my life in purity and to practice my profession faithfully. I will abstain from whatever is deleterious and mischievous and will not take or knowingly administer any harmful drug. I will do all in my power to elevate the standard of my profession and will hold in confidence all personal matters committed to my keeping and all family affairs coming to my knowledge in the practice of my calling. With loyalty will I endeavor to aid the physician in his work and devote myself to the welfare of those committed to my care [Editorial, 1911, p. 596].

I liked the sound of the newest word to my vocabulary and said it repeatedly to get the accent and inflection just right—

del-e-ter-i-ous. I could honestly pledge to refrain from harmful acts in caring for patients but wondered if I could abstain from being mischievous with my peers.

Why the pledge? In 1893, a special committee at Harper Hospital in Detroit, Michigan, prepared a nurse pledge and named it after Florence Nightingale. She knew nothing of the pledge until she received a copy from the authors after its creation. The Michigan nurse leaders chose the Nightingale name as a token of esteem for her. This pledge, which was revised in 1935, was used in schools of nursing for many years. Portions of the original pledge were retained in the updated terminology of nurse practice acts of the 1980s and 1990s (Calhoun, 1993).

During the war years, pre-cadets often repeated both the Corps and the Nightingale Pledges as part of the capping ceremony. When the war ended cadets no longer pledged to remain in active nursing for the duration of the war.

Why the cap? The origin of the nurse's cap goes back to medieval times when the bridal veil symbolized a woman's humility and obedience (Jamieson & Sewell, 1942). In England, as with any properly dressed lady, Florence Nightingale always wore her cap when indoors or her bonnet when she went out. Queen Victoria set the fashion for her day wearing a plain stiffened muslin cap with pleated edging. Later nurses covered their hair with a cap to promote hygiene for the patient ("Why a Cap," 1940). The nurse's cap was also a symbol of service to humanity. By 1900 the cap no longer served merely as a covering for the hair but also became the nurses' symbol. Ways of wearing the caps often reflected other social trends. For example, when short hair became popular, nurses positioned their caps to complement the new styles.

All student nurses at the University of Minnesota wore the same style of white cap so patients could not tell if students were junior or senior cadets. (However, graduate nurses received a distinctively different cap.) Cadet Albina Borho Reichmuth fondly remembered, "The solemn capping ceremony was held in the Powell Hall Lounge and included singing, a speech by Miss Densford, the dean of the school of nursing, and a reception. I was thrilled when Miss Densford placed the cap on my head.

A cadet nurse from a Kentucky school of nursing said:

> Capping ceremony? It didn't happen for our class. Cadets gathered in the library where the director handed out the caps and bibs. The stern superintendent of nurses said, "Now you know what the nursing world is all about. If you are unable to cope, I suggest you check out."

Alice Jans Donley of the Sioux Valley Hospital of Nursing in Sioux Falls, South Dakota, experienced great joy in passing the probation period. No longer would she have to wear the black bow tie that set her apart as a probation student. As the only probie proficient at tying a bow, she performed this procedure on the black ties of her classmates who lined up before her every morning.

In preparation for the evening capping ceremony, the pre-cadets shined their black shoes, pulled on their black stockings, and put on their sharp, crisp blue and white striped student uniforms. They got in a line with their Florence Nightingale lamps and marched to the front of the auditorium to receive their starched, beautiful, white nursing caps. "I shall never forget the symbolic experience of capping and the lighting of the lamps," Alice said.

For quite a different reason, Mary Wilcox Foster remembered her capping ceremony at Robert Packer Hospital School of Nursing in Sayre, Pennsylvania. After the ceremony, impressive with the solemn lighting of the "Spirit of Nursing" candles, the newly capped cadets filed out of the church. As she came down the church steps, the garter broke on one of her stockings. Then the second garter came loose and both stockings slowly slipped down her legs. "There I was, grabbing for my stockings," Mary said. Fortunately her friends gathered around, shielding her from view, as she hobbled back to the nurses' residence clutching her stockings.

Betty Jane Kent Bodin from St. Luke's Hospital School of Nursing in Duluth, Minnesota, told of another aspect of the significance of the nurse cap when she said: "Taking away the coveted cap was an effective means of punishment for making a mistake. We proudly wore our nurse caps as we gave patient care in the hospital wards. If a cadet made a medication or treatment error, she was not allowed to wear her cap for as long as a month. Thus everyone knew when we made errors."

Why uniforms? The use of uniforms by schools of nursing in America evolved from a need for uniformity, cleanliness, and economy, while maintaining militaristic control of the student nurses (Jamieson & Sewall, 1942). The probationary and preclinical students of many schools of nursing, especially those with religious affiliations, wore all white uniforms. At other schools the uniforms were dresses of striped fabric or of fabric in plain colors such as blue, pink, brown, or green. At many schools variations included an apron or bib worn over the basic uniform. White or black shoes and stockings completed the student nurse uniform for hospital duty.

Betty Deming Pearson's story about uniforms shows another perspective.

> We wore the same medium blue cotton uniforms for the entire program at the University of Minnesota except that the medium blue turned to faded blue by the time we became senior cadets.
>
> "Button, button, who's got the button?" [This] might well have been the chant of the pre-cadets. There were buttons down the front of the blue dress, buttons on the cuffs, buttons on the self-belt, and buttons on the tabard style apron. With all those shank buttons removed for laundering, it took 15 minutes to set up a clean uniform. A black washable tie ... in a Windsor knot, tucked between the second and third buttons of the bodice completed the uniform.

Despite the differences in colors of student uniforms from one school to another, consistency prevailed in one area. At many schools of nursing in the 1940s the ritual of nurses wearing white at graduation was observed.

Added to the uniforms of the student nurses were name badges. If a newly capped cadet at Lincoln General Hospital of Nursing had the same last name as a junior or senior cadet, a first initial was added to the nametag of the newly capped cadet. For instance, my classmate, Phyllis Wright Cerney, and I had name tags that included our first initials: Miss P. Morey and Miss P. Wright. Cadet chums dubbed us P. More and P. Right. Although we silently shrank from the titles, pride kept us from showing that it bothered us.

Capping or striping ceremonies and graduation signified accomplishments in the lives of cadet nurses. But other rituals, some official and some unofficial, affected cadet lives as well.

Morning chapel became a special ritual for pre-cadets in many schools of nursing. Edith Tullis Olsen recalled, "[Administrators] of the General Hospital School of Nursing in Madison, Wisconsin, required our attendance at chapel before we went on duty by 8:00 a.m. or to early class." When the cadet nurses walked down the hallway to the auditorium, a supervisor conducted a weekly uniform inspection, checking for unpolished shoes, dirty shoestrings, messy uniforms, or caps improperly folded. The teacher in charge kept a record and reprimanded offenders.

Edith also recalled that at the chapel service cadets were expected to repeat the Lord's Prayer and sing hymns. The leader especially liked "Eternal Father, Strong to Save," the Navy hymn that went like this:

> Eternal Father, strong to save,
> Whose arm hath bound the restless wave,
> Who biddest the mighty ocean deep
> Its own appointed limits keep;
> O hear us when we cry to Thee
> For those in peril on the sea!
> (Whiting, 1860)

"We laughed at the words," Edith said, "for we cadets thought we needed prayers as much as the sailors."

Ursula Hanson Hawkins remembered other events that had special meaning.

We all looked forward to two great days at the University of Minnesota: "Ripping Day" and "Finishing Day." Ripping Day occurred on the last day that we wore the blue student uniform, which was faded and mended from frequent harsh launderings. Classmates met us in the hall as we left duty, cutting and ripping the uniforms to shreds. We had to remember to wear a slip that day.

On Finishing Day we wore the white uniforms and new graduate caps for the first time. The honoree and friends proceeded to the cafeteria where there was a decorated cake on the tea table. The new nurse received a corsage and other surprises. Because of make-up time no two nurses ever finished on the same day.

Everyone on the units knew the date of Mary Petersen Claybourn's Ripping Day and they fiendishly ripped off her sleeves and tore her uniform. When her student uniform hung in shreds, she put on a patient gown for the rest of the shift. "Some of the students took their torn uniforms and threw them into the Mississippi River from the Washington Avenue Bridge," Mary recalled.

The rituals of the schools of nursing provided an incentive for cadets to keep moving ahead. Each addition or change to the uniform, which was a symbol of progression through the nursing hierarchy, encouraged cadets to keep their eyes on the higher goal of becoming a registered nurse.

Romps

The rituals supplied rewards as we traveled down the path to reach our goals, but the romps made it fun getting there. As teenagers and young adults, full of energy and fun, we romped and rollicked to balance the weight of trust and duty placed on us.

Having fun also provided the cadets with a way to cope. Anne Higgins Murphy described the importance of the fun and rollicking when she said:

We cadet nurses at Flower-Fifth Avenue Hospital School of Nursing in New York City laughed a lot, for having good friends made it easier to endure our trials and anxieties. The Big Apple with its museums, theaters, big department stores, Yankee Stadium and many different restaurants, churches, and concerts provided a variety of activities for young people who served in World War II.

Best of all we appreciated the abundance of dates but because of the war years our friendships often ended when a military group shipped out.

Helen Harris Engle, who attended Tacoma General Hospital School of Nursing, also described the importance of friendships as a way to cope during difficult times when she said:

We went to Point Defiance Park in the State of Washington, where we rode horses on the forest trails or rowed a boat out on Puget Sound for 50 cents an hour. We loved the park with its rose gardens, miles of trails, beach for swimming, the zoo and the aquarium. The cooks at the hospital packed box lunches for cadets and their dates going on day outings.

The large army post and naval installations nearby provided cadets with plenty of young, available, uniformed men for good times during off duty hours. Cadets in their snappy gray uniforms with silver buttons and red epaulets danced with servicemen at the USO on a regular basis and viewed the latest movies. "None of us had cars nor did the servicemen whom we dated," Helen said.

Cadets in Wheeling, West Virginia, also enjoyed some good times. According to Eleanor White O'Niel:

My years at Ohio Valley General Hospital School of Nursing in Wheeling, West Virginia, meant hard work and study. Cadets had little money but joked and talked in each other's rooms. After pooling our money, one of the cadets ran down the hill to buy a big bag of raised doughnuts. Oh, they tasted so good.

We also walked to town to window shop and in the summer caught the streetcar, crossing Wheeling Island into Ohio then returning to West Virginia, all for 10 cents. We laughed and sang and the other passengers laughed too, either with us or at us, I'm not sure which.

Each class at the Henry Ford Hospital School of Nursing in Detroit, Michigan, took a turn providing monthly entertainment. Molly Sharrard Dailey described one such event.

> Our freshman class prepared a musical program complete with costumes that progressed from the Gay Nineties through World War I, the Roaring '20s, and World War II. The 10-cent admission fee went to the March of Dimes.
>
> We invited long-term patients to our productions and many patients watched from their wheel chairs and stretchers. Dr. McClure, chief of staff, impressed with the show, requested a private showing and invited Mr. and Mrs. Henry Ford. We added, *Jeanie With the Light Brown Hair*, Mr. Ford's favorite song and presented our command performance to Mr. and Mrs. Ford, Dr. McClure, and Miss Moran, director of nurses, who were all seated in easy chairs.

According to Mary Tamplen Rupel, at the Lubbock General Hospital School of Nursing in Texas, cadet nurses did not have much spare time so they enjoyed it to the fullest. Mary and other cadets dated officers from the army airfield or the glider pilot training school and attended their dances and other activities. They bowled, picnicked in the park, or went to the movies. If cadets worked night duty or could not go out for the evening, their dates often brought their buddies along and the cadets and the servicemen talked, sang, or danced in the living room of the nurses' residence. "Almost all of them were single and lonely being away from their homes and loved ones," said Mary.

Some of the activities the cadets enjoyed were at the local universities and colleges. Barbara Oetzel Lenthart told this story:

> Although Madison General Hospital School of Nursing did not [have an official affiliation] with the University of Wisconsin, cadet nurses enjoyed social activities at the university. We attended sporting events, concerts, and lectures and relaxed in the student union. When in Madison we walked; we walked on dates, we walked to church, we walked to the movie.

Cadets with no nearby military installations went to other places where the men were-the train station. "We walked to the depot to meet the troop trains when they stopped in Sayre, Pennsylvania," Harriet McCann Kellogg said. Occasionally one of the service personnel received treatment at Robert Packer Hospital. One soldier who had an emergency appendectomy thought he awoke in heaven because of all the attention he received from the cadets.

"We dated in groups," Harriet remembered, "and pooled our resources to take our dates to dinner. When the bill arrived and exceeded the amount of our funds, we borrowed money from our dates."

Cadet Hilda Morrison Harned in Minot, North Dakota who was enrolled at the Trinity Hospital School of Nursing stated:

> We walked more than a mile in severe winter weather to greet the GIs at the USO. We saved money from our stipends and ate downtown as often as funds allowed. [Eating downtown] was a welcome relief from hospital food. My weekly letter from mother included a silver dime, just the amount for admission to my favorite movies featuring Van Johnson and June Allyson.

The senior cadet nurses assigned to the Portsmouth U.S. Naval Base, Portsmouth, Virginia, in 1944 had an advocate in Lt. Commander Leola R. Scheips, chief naval liaison officer for the Cadet Nurse Corps. "Those cadet nurses showed commitment to giving service," retired Lt. Scheips LeBar recalled. In response to their effort, she organized a program for cadet nurses who did not have officers' social privileges and sponsored a weekly tea in the officers' quarters. She said, "Chatting over a tea cup gave us an opportunity to discuss the military aspects and social problems affecting cadet nurses."

Betty Cheney Sexton, a cadet at the University of Colorado School of Nursing, told a story about the unusual events that could occur when taking a vacation or going to an affiliate agency while wearing the cadet uniform.

The U.S. Cadet Nurse Corps Band of St. Mary's Hospital School of Nursing in Huntington, West Virginia, tuned up for some lively music. Other groups sponsored by the school were drama, literary, music appreciation, recreation, and glee clubs.

> When I wore the Cadet Nurse Corps uniform most people could not distinguish me from the members of the regular armed forces. One time I went to Union Station in Denver to buy a train ticket to go home between quarters. I presented the ticket agent with the regular fee. Seeing my cadet uniform the ticket agent said, "You get furlough rates."
>
> I questioned if I was truly eligible for a discounted train fare, but the agent, adamant and busy, hurried me along. I paid the 75 cents discounted train fare and boarded the train, crowded with servicemen. I sat in the aisle on my suitcase the entire distance to Grand Junction, Colorado, but I didn't mind because of the money I saved.

A cadet nurse from the Frances Payne Bolton School of Nursing in Cleveland, Ohio, recalled that she paid dearly for wearing her cadet uniform to take advantage of a military discount. On her first big vacation, a 5-day train trip to California, she said that while changing trains in the Dearborn station in Chicago, she heard the announcement, "Is there a doctor or nurse in the station?" Two military policemen dragged an unconscious lady and a toddler to the cadet and laid the prone woman in front of her. The cadet had been in nursing for only 6 months so could hardly fake an air of confidence as she took the lady's pulse.

"When the MPs went for a gurney, I served the most good by keeping the toddler from getting lost in the passing crowd," the cadet said, "rather than anything I did to help the patient." She stayed with the lady and toddler in the first aid station until an ambulance arrived.

The uncertainty generated when members of the Corps were confused with members of the military services prompted Corps Director Lucile Petry to issue memorandum #25 dated July 24, 1944, to the directors of the schools of nursing concerning furlough forms for U.S. Cadets:

> Some members of the U.S. Cadet Nurse Corps have encountered transportation difficulties (when ticket agents requested furlough papers).... We are printing forms which will be sent in the near future. If you will announce the availability of these forms and give them, (signed) on request, to cadet nurses who are traveling in uniform, it will clarify the situation for any agent, who in line of duty, might question their right to travel (Petry, 1940).

Cadet nurses learned to balance the problems of life, birth, and death with the enthusiasm of youth and the yearning for self-expression, joy, and release. The romps and rollicks of their teenage years helped the cadets cope with the solemn responsibility of holding lives in their hands.

References

Calhoun, J. (1993). Nightingale pledge: A commitment that survives the passage of time. **Nursing and Healthcare, 14**(3), 130-135.

Editorial. (1911). **American Journal of Nursing, 11**(5), 596.

Jamieson, E.M., & Sewall, M. (1942). Trends in nursing history (pp. 430-432). Philadelphia: Saunders.

Petry, L. (1940). **Furlough forms for U.S. Cadets.** (Memorandum #25). USPHS. [RG 90]. Washington, DC: National Archives and Records Administration.

Whiting, W. (1860). Eternal father, strong to save, (Hymn Stanza 1). In **Armed Forces Hymnal,** 1963 (p. 390). USGPO.

Why a cap? (1940). **American Journal of Nursing, 40**(4), 384-386.

9

There's A War On
by Paulie M. Perry

Across the nation, cadets and their families did their parts to support the war effort. In Kansas, the geographical center of the nation, the Morey family participated in V-mail, victory gardens, rationing, and recycling; and endured censorship and shortages. V-mail was initiated by the postal service to conserve on the weight of mail sent back and forth between military personnel and civilians. The officials recognized the importance of the mail for boosting morale. Letters were written on special V-mail forms, which were then photographed, reduced in size, and mailed to recipients. Censoring was also part of the process. Military personnel mailed letters without charge by writing the word "free" in the space designated for stamps.

Victory gardens were encouraged in order to supplement the national food supply. Patriotic citizens across the United States planted fruit and vegetable gardens in window boxes, alleys, vacant lots, and former flowerbeds.

We abided by the rationing regulations on sugar, gasoline, and shoes. We curtailed travel and drove at the specified 35 miles per hour speed limit to save wear and tear on tires. If neighbors squealed tires and drove too fast, someone chided them saying, "Don't you know there's a war on?"

Wally, the only boy of our Morey family, volunteered for the Navy in June 1942 and Thelma, one of the girls, became a member of the U.S. Cadet Nurse Corps in 1943. Friends and neighbors, especially those like the Moreys who had family members in the military, were fiercely patriotic. They shared news of their servicemen and women, where they were stationed, when they would come home on leave, and the theater of war in which they served. Family members eagerly searched the daily mail for letters, often to be disappointed.

The short supply of farm hands prompted the high school officials in our area to dismiss school for a week in the fall of 1944 so that students could help with the corn harvest. I loved this working vacation and became adept at shucking corn, snapping off the ears and throwing them against the "bang board" so they would fall into the wagon. The horses, trained to follow the rows of corn as they pulled the wagon from one end of the field to the other, jerked off ears of corn to munch while they plodded along.

Family life became segmented as parents and children were separated. Eligible young men served in the armed services and young women joined a variety of uniformed services or worked in essential wartime jobs. Many married women entered the work force and often parents worked different shifts, doing their part on the home front. In the windows of

Dad's helper headed for the farm fields in Kansas to help alleviate the farm labor shortage. Paulie Morey (Perry) was one of many high school students across the nation who helped with the harvest of various agricultural products during the war years.

their homes, families displayed red, white, and blue banners with a star for each family member in the service. Sometimes the star was gold, which meant a son or daughter had died for our country.

Camilla Ecklund Johnson and her family went through trying times in the early and mid '40s. When Camilla was a high school senior at the university-sponsored Agricultural School of Crookston, Minnesota, she received news that her oldest brother had died from injuries sustained in a neighborhood game of ice hockey on the Red River.

Later, in 1945 senior cadet nurse Camilla, serving at the Seattle Naval Base Hospital, was shocked when she received the message that her only living brother was killed in action in the Battle of Leyte in the Philippines. "The news devastated me but crushed my parents even more having lost all three sons, the first as an infant who succumbed to pneumonia."

Now with all their sons gone, the family had no one to carry on the Ecklund name or take over the family farm in northern Minnesota. But they coped with their grief and lived a full and productive life despite the hurt in their hearts. Camilla endured the pain of her military brother's death while being so far away from friends and family because another cadet nurse had received similar news concerning her brother. "We supported each other," Camilla said.

A story told by a Kentucky cadet nurse indicates the kind of life that cadet came from, the worry she had to endure, and how the Corps made a difference in her life.

The army reported my brother, an early enlistee, missing in action during the African campaign. Six months passed before the army notified the family that my brother was a prisoner in one of the stalags [camps] in Germany. An additional agonizing 3 months went by before they heard directly from him confirming he was alive.

Probably no area of the USA changed more than Appalachia in World War II. The young people left in a mass exodus, either to the military or for jobs in the cities. My father, who served as chairman of the county draft board and as county superintendent of the state highway department, dealt with a lack of qualified employees.

My mother, a former teacher, not only knitted for the war effort but also wrote letters for illiterate mothers to their sons in the service. She taught coal miners' wives how to substitute sorghum molasses and honey for rationed sugar and how to can or dehydrate fruits and vegetables grown in their hillside victory gardens.

This young woman graduated from college at 17 and taught health and physical education in a mining camp school, saving money to leave Appalachia. "I was working as a technician in the animal laboratory of a pharmaceutical company when the plant nurse told me about the Cadet Nurse Corps," she said. "With my brother a prisoner of war, I wanted to contribute to the war effort so it seemed appropriate to join the Corps."

The Corps provided the opportunity for her to continue her education. She chose a graduate-school nursing program and graduated in 1944 with a master's degree.

More than 575 enrollees in the U.S. Cadet Nurse Corps stood on the steps of the Los Angeles County General Hospital in May 1944. It was one of the largest training groups of its kind in the United States. As cadets graduated and became registered nurses, they chose military or civilian duty.

Another cadet, Patricia Ruby Morse told how she and her family contributed to the war effort. "Dad served as an air raid warden for our block and we participated in war bond drives in my home town of Cedar Rapids, Iowa."

My mother collected bacon drippings and donated them for the manufacture of explosives. Bare legs were the norm because dressy stockings were scarce. Silk had a Japanese connotation and nylon was scarce because it was used to make parachutes. Because gas was rationed and was scarce for family use, father would not teach my sister or me to drive the family car.

The citizens dimmed streetlights and store windows to obey blackout orders. I did not have a radio, nor did many of my friends, so we relied on the newspaper for reports from the war fronts. The news did not include weather reports, as this might assist the enemy. We never knew the extent of the cold Iowa nights.

As the oldest of my family I had wanted to be a nurse from the age of 10. When I checked on schools of nursing, my mother asked, "Where do you think the $50 tuition is coming from?" I learned about the Cadet Nurse Corps through the girls' dean at high school. Thus the Corps provided the financial support I needed.

"We endured shortages of coffee, sugar, gasoline, and hosiery," Donna Hardenburger Kennedy remembered. "But everyone was in the same boat and we didn't complain." When preparing to enter Lincoln General Hospital School of Nursing in September of 1944, she found electric irons were scarce, but after much shopping she discovered and purchased a used iron in a second-hand store. Finding it impossible to buy a new watch with a second-hand, Donna used one of her dad's pocket watches. "I hung it on a shoe string and wore it around my neck," she said.

In July 1944 Corps Director Lucile Petry, issued memo #28 to schools of nursing, which disclosed the good news that watches with second-hands would soon be available (Petry, 1944). About 75,000 wristwatches, manufactured especially for use by nurses, were released by the War Production Board to be sold through local jewelers. The purchaser need only have proper identification as a nurse or nurse aide. The Office of Price Administration (OPA) established $5 as the price ceiling ("Wrist Watches," 1944).

According to Dorothie Melvin Crowley, "World War II put a damper on life in Long Beach, California."

Automobile factories produced airplanes and tanks for the duration of the war. This meant no new cars. My mother took classes in the Douglas Aircraft School, learned to use a transit, read blueprints, and worked at Douglas in the layout department until the war ended. My mother's going to work added to the vast changes in our family schedules. Family members worked irregular hours and relatives, caught in the housing shortage, frequently "camped out" with us.

After high school graduation in June of 1943 a friend and I attended a local junior college. It was wartime and we felt the urge to do something useful. A poster of a cadet nurse impressed us and we inquired [at] schools of nursing in the area about how to become a cadet nurse. We met all the requirements except for chemistry and we made that up at the local junior college. So began my career for a lifetime, thanks to the Corps.

"We were fortunate as a family because although several cousins served in different branches of service, none gave his life," said Cadet Edith Tullis Olsen. Living in Evansville, Wisconsin, they had no blackouts but did face the challenges of rationed meat, sugar, coffee, shoes, and gasoline.

My mother, widowed when my father died in an automobile accident in 1938, got a job as clerk in the men's department of a clothing store because no men were available. The men were either in essential civilian work or in military service. This proved to be a turning point for our family because it meant we now had an adequate income and it raised mother's self esteem tremendously.

Following high school graduation, I worked as a secretary in Madison, Wisconsin, for a boss who made my life miserable. Although I was unhappy, I strove to be a success. Then along came the Cadet Nurse Corps. Here was a way for me to help others, study to become a nurse, and have my education paid for. My twin sister and I applied at Madison General Hospital School of Nursing.

The school had been closed for 6 years because of inadequate facilities and fewer patients during the Depression. In view of the desperate need for nurses, a new nurses' dormitory and a classroom building were built, with one class already in session. After cramming our way through a chemistry course at the vocational school and passing our physicals, both of us were accepted in the March class. A lifetime education was fulfilled for me.

Another cadet came to Madison General under far different circumstances. "The army drafted my oldest brother soon after war broke out in Europe," said Alice Noguchi Kanagaki. After Japan bombed Pearl Harbor, life changed severely for Alice's family and others of Japanese ancestry.

Because the town of Martinez, a county seat and railroad center, was near a naval shipyard, my "alien" parents were ordered to move to a nonvital zone at Concord, California. They lived in a friend's garage while two of my brothers and I stayed in Martinez to run the family store.

When Executive Order #9066 was issued on February 19, 1942, the U.S. Government relocated 110,000 Japanese-Americans (Maddox, 1992). Those financially able moved to the Midwest or East Coast. The rest were sent to barbwire-fenced relocation camps, guarded by armed soldiers. In March 1942 the government moved Alice, her family, and other relatives to temporary housing in Turlock, California. They were fortunate to be located in barracks because other Japanese lived in horse stables, one family per stall. Five months later they were transferred to quarters at the Gila, Arizona, relocation camp.

As Alice neared high school graduation in May 1944 her cousin, a student at Madison General Hospital School of Nursing in Wisconsin, told her about the Cadet Nurse Corps. "This was welcome news," Alice said, "for we had no income and no money for schooling."

I mailed an application to Madison General and was one of the last to be accepted for the fall class. The school accepted me on the merits of my cousin's outstanding scholastic record.

I graduated in September of 1947. I devoted 36 years to nursing, making good use of the education provided by the Cadet Nurse Corps.

Eleanor Wade Smagala tells another story about how she became a cadet. Both of Eleanor's parents served in World War I, her father in the Navy and her mother as an Army nurse.

Although a busy farmer's wife raising a family, mother helped neighbors with medical emergencies and home deliveries. During World War II she returned to full-time nursing because of the nurse shortage.

White Pigeon, a patriotic town in Michigan, honored its veterans-for the most part. I found it ironic that the town never remembered mother on Memorial Day even though she endured months of hardships near the front lines in France during World War I.

Coming from a service-minded family and influenced from an early age to believe nurses not only helped people but also could always find a job, Eleanor found the Cadet Nurse Corps a perfect blend. In July 1944 she took a bus to Highland Park (Michigan) General Hospital School of Nursing for an interview and physical exam. "What a happy day on August 14th when I received the letter notifying me I was accepted," Eleanor said.

Cadets due to graduate in early 1945 faced the possible decision of joining the service or being subject to the nurse draft being proposed at that time. In his state of the union message on January 6, 1945, President Franklin Delano Roosevelt shocked the nation when he said:

Since volunteering has not produced the number of nurses required, I urge the Selective Service Act be amended to provide for induction of nurses into the armed forces. The need is too pressing to await the outcome of further efforts at recruiting (Kalisch & Kalisch, 1973, pp. 403-410).

Some citizens wondered what had happened to the surplus of nurses in the '30s. With the entry of the United States into the war in 1941, volunteer enlistment rose to sufficient levels, but by 1943 "war weariness" had set in. The Battle of the Bulge in Belgium in December 1944 brought the heaviest casualties of the war-1,750 each day. The need for nurses quickly became acute. Secretary of War Henry L. Stimson received approval for drastic action from President Roosevelt— a draft of female nurses. Two legislative assistants worked on the proposed bill through Christmas Eve.

The day following President Roosevelt's call for a draft of nurses, Katharine Densford, president of the American Nurses Association, stated she was convinced his message would result in an immediate increase in the number of volunteers. Stella Goostray, president of the National Nursing Council for War Service, appealed to nurses to enlist at once, pending legislation. This was the first and only time in its history that the U.S. government asked for a draft that discriminated in respect to occupation ("Proposed Draft," 1945).

On February 6, 1945, Surgeon General Thomas Parran of the USPHS reported to the House Committee on Military Affairs. He said the best estimates indicated cadet nurses were giving 80% of the nursing care in associated hospitals. The cadet nurses had responded for military duty in much greater proportion than did their classmates, who were not in the Corps. The surgeon general said, "As the war progresses, the major civilian health problems are still ahead of us. We shall see the cumulative effects of fatigue, long hours of work, worry, anxiety, and grief (Parran, 1945, p. 995).

Bill HR 2277, the Nurse Draft, reached the house floor March 5, 1945, following passionate debate. One of the provisions of the bill stated no nurse would be drafted until all available graduates of the United States Cadet Nurse Corps had been inducted.

Some congressmen argued that because cadet nurses received their education at federal expense, they had a special obligation to serve their country. Others stated the provision was unjust because cadets had pledged to remain in either civilian or military nursing after graduation. The proposal failed and on March 7, 1945, an amended bill passed the House by a record vote of 347 to 42 and moved on to the Senate (Kalisch & Kalisch, 1973).

Also in March, Allied forces crossed the Rhine River into Germany and General Patton's troops captured Frankfurt; Congress began to doubt the necessity for drafting nurses. With victory seemingly closer, last-ditch efforts for recruitment were successful. Nurses, under pressure of a pending draft, responded with 10,000 applications for commissions within a 3-week period. Rumors of a draft stimulated 60% of senior cadet nurses to choose military instead of civilian employment. Civilian hospitals resourcefully added older nurses to their staffs (Kalisch & Kalisch, 1973).

By V-E Day (Victory in Europe) on May 8, 1945, the supply of nurses for postwar Germany exceeded the need, and the surgeon general's office recommended that the war department cease pressing for legislation to draft nurses. The Senate dropped the proposed nurse draft bill, a gratifying result of Allied military successes (Kalisch & Kalisch, 1973).

During spring, 1945, Irene Endres Browning was one of those cadets who answered the call to volunteer. She said:

> I joined the Army inspired by my sister who spent 3 years in Naples, Italy, as an Army surgical nurse. After graduating from St. Camillius Borgess Hospital School of Nursing in Kalamazoo, Michigan, I exchanged my cadet nurse uniform for that of an army nurse fulfilling my pledge as a cadet. I received orders for assignment to the Percy Jones Army Hospital in Battle Creek, Michigan, then on to Fort Bragg, North Carolina, where the army trained me for overseas duty. I served in Breman and Frankfurt, Germany, returning to the states in October 1946, proud to have served my country first as a cadet, and then as an Army nurse.

Cadets form a V for victory, not only in their formation on the steps of Creighton Memorial St. Joseph Hospital in Omaha, Nebraska, but also in their hearts as they pledged to remain in nursing for the duration of World War II.

"As the war went on and on, we knew cadet nurses faced the possibility of being drafted," recalled Ruth Olson Stapleton of the University of Minnesota School of Nursing. When the end of the war in Europe stopped proposals to draft nurses, Ruth had a choice when she graduated in June 1945. After she made up her missed time, she could either return home and become a staff nurse in northern Minnesota or continue her education at the university. Ruth chose to remain at the university hospital where she accepted a position as assistant head nurse. She shared an apartment with four classmates until she and her fiancé, a veteran attending the University of Minnesota on the G.I. Bill, could afford to get married.

World War II united citizens across the length and breadth of the nation in a common cause-winning the war. Women answered the call to duty with many joining the Corps and fulfilling their obligation in either civilian or military nursing. Yes, the cadet nurses knew there was a war on. They proudly served their country.

References

Kalisch, P.A., & Kalisch, B.J. (1973, September-October).The women's draft. **Nursing Research,** 403-410.
Maddox, R.J. (1992). **The United States and World War II** (pp. 197-198). Boulder, CO: Westview Press.
Parran. T. (1945). The cadet nurse corps. **JAMA, 127**(15), 995.
Petry, L. (1994, July 24). **Watches with second hands.** (Memorandum #28, USPHS, Division of Nurse Education). (RG 90). Washington, DC: National Archives and Records Administration.
Proposed draft of nurses. Editorial.(1945). **American Journal of Nursing, 45**(2), 87.
Wristwatches for nurses. (1944). **American Journal of Nursing, 44**(12), 1189.

10

Serving While Learning: The Junior Cadet
by Thelma M. Robinson

In 1943 nurse leader Stella Goostray, president of the National League of Nursing Education, addressed the American Association's Second War Conference in Buffalo, New York, saying, "[T]he effective use of student nurse power in the present emergency and preparation for the postwar nursing requires that we maintain the essential elements of a sound preparation" (Goostray, 1943, p. 67). She advised administrators of schools of nursing to use pruning shears where there was overlapping and repetition in the curriculum but to maintain the essentials of good preparation for nursing.

Cadet nurses advanced to junior status after the 9-month pre-cadet period and remained in this grade for the next 21 months. During this time, cadet nurses attended classes and staffed the wards while learning the four basic services: medical, surgical, pediatric, and obstetric. The $15 stipend received by pre-cadet nurses increased to $20 each month for junior cadet nurses ("Laws Authorizing," 1943). Thus junior cadet nurses served while they learned. What do former cadet nurses remember about those times?

Cadet nurses attending the Frances Payne Bolton School of Nursing in Cleveland, Ohio, received a small food allowance. Paying directly for their meals in the hospital cafeteria was a financial burden for many junior cadets. A graduate of this program said, "We had no money left for frivolity. With the help of upper classmate friends, we soon learned to steal sanitary pads from the obstetrics unit and snitch food from the diet kitchen."

The dormitory switchboard operator at the Frances Payne Bolton school ran a baby-sitter service. Student nurses could earn 35 cents an hour before midnight and 50 cents for each hour thereafter for babysitting. This extra money provided significant financial help to the cadets as well as allowing quiet time for study or contemplation after the children were tucked into bed. As a cadet nurse from Ohio thought back on this period of her life, she recalled that hardly anyone could afford radios or record players. The only opportunity to read a newspaper was to quickly glance at headlines while at a patient's bedside or during the time at a baby-sitting job. "After the children were in bed, I enjoyed the family's classical record collection, the radio, newspapers, and magazines," she said.

Junior cadet nurses checked off new nursing procedures learned in their record books, pleased to learn more involved methods of caring for their patients. Junior cadets continued to give bed baths before medical rounds and carried basins of warm water to patients' bedsides for evening care. They massaged backs before bedtime, passed medications and

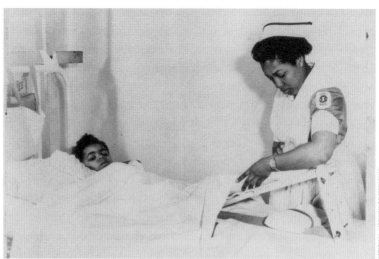

NATIONAL LIBRARY OF MEDICINE

A cadet nurse from Freedmen's Hospital in Washington, DC, adjusts traction on a child.

administered complicated treatments. To accomplish these nursing tasks, cadet nurses were assigned a strange combination of hours in a day:

7- 9 a.m. and 1-7 p.m.

7-11 a.m. and 7-11 p.m.

7-11 a.m. and 3-7 p.m.

7 a.m.-1 p.m. and 5-7 p.m.

These split shifts were an economic strategy for hospital service, saving on the cost of nursing, but were killers for cadet nurses who also had classes during their "off" hours.

Who cared for the patients when the students vacated the wards leaving only the charge nurse? Often it was volunteers. In the grave wartime need for nurses, the American Red Cross trained thousands of volunteer nurses. Mrs. McConnell, a minister's wife, typical of the many women who answered this call, attended an 80-hour Red Cross Nurse's Aide course. Then she gave thousands of hours to helping patients in the hospital in her community (McConnell, 1942).

As junior cadet nurses at Lincoln General Hospital, we depended upon Mrs. McConnell to bridge the gap in nursing care while we attended class. When we returned to the ward, Mrs. McConnell greeted us. Her face was flushed and beads of perspiration glistened on her brow from racing up and down the corridors answering call lights. Always pleasant and smiling, she reported to us about our patients. This generous woman and thousands of volunteer Red Cross aides like her performed a vital service without pay in the struggle to cope with a critical nurse shortage.

Cadet Nurse Corps regulations limited the cadets' work to no more than 48 hours each week including classes attended. However, because of the extreme shortage of nurses, cadets frequently exceeded those 48 hours. Cadet nurses who worked late evening and nights often fell asleep during their daytime classes. Cadet Dorothy Luther, at Duke University School of Nursing in North Carolina, recalled the chief of orthopedics throwing chalk at a student nurse he caught napping in his class.

Later in Dorothy's nursing career she became a professor of nursing and taught 100 or more undergraduate and graduate nursing students at the Universities of Florida and Kentucky. She explained the nursing curriculum in the '40s:

> The physicians taught the nurse classes but the Nursing Education director graded the tests. At the end of each unit, the nursing supervisor discussed the nursing care of the type of patient being described. When the doctors taught nurse classes we learned more about pathology, differential diagnosis, and medical therapies than about nursing care.

About this time streptomycin and penicillin became available in limited quantities for only a few patients. Cadet nurses remembered the miraculous cures. "Two little black boys who had contacted tularemia while rabbit hunting were admitted to my ward and successfully treated with streptomycin. Previously, without exception, this disease was fatal," Dorothy said.

Claribel Carlson Crews from Lincoln General Hospital School of Nursing in Nebraska recalled caring for a young farmer who was critically ill and emaciated from bacterial endocarditis, a heart disease. The physicians obtained penicillin in a beeswax suspension for him. The dosage of 5 cc (a little more than 1 teaspoonful) was given intramuscularly with a large-gauge needle every 3 hours. The beeswax slowed the absorption. Frequent doses were necessary because the earlier forms of penicillin were excreted rapidly. Gastric juices destroyed the potency of the medication so it could not be given by mouth (Keefer, 1943).

> The poor man had little muscle in which to give the injection. The assistant head nurse gave the penicillin while I offered moral support to both the nurse and the patient. I will never forget the patient's tears and the nurse's as well. The experience was devastating for all of us but our patient walked out of the hospital recovered from his illness. Penicillin was a wonder drug. Life in the hospital became an exciting place as new medicines became available.

Sterilizing materials took a lot of nurses' time in the 1940s. In the photo above, a "scrubbed" nurse unloads the autoclave while a cadet nurse observes.

Cadet nurses cleaned equipment for reuse because almost nothing was disposable then. Dorothie Melvin Crowley remembered washing intravenous (IV) bottles on the wards, then taking them to central supply for further cleaning. Eight hours of continuously running water was used to rinse the special tubing used for administering blood. Hospital personnel prepared IV solutions and refilled previously used IV bottles with the solution. The bottles were then placed in the autoclave to be sterilized with steam under pressure.

Cadet nurses wrestled with the heavy oxygen tanks and often went off duty with rust-stained uniforms. All personnel needed to be vigilant when transporting large oxygen cylinders to the bedsides of patients and while strapping the tanks to the beds. They also had to:

- "crack" (partially open) the value to remove dust particles and prevent damage to the flow meter;
- watch the regulator to assure that a steady stream of oxygen flowed to the patient;
- ensure that patients and visitors did not smoke.

Cadet Nurse Deloris Giltner who attended Seton School of Nursing in Colorado Springs remembered the following about the use of oxygen, "We were cautioned that if an oxygen tank fell over, the heavy metal cylinder could explode. One night a tank fell over but, thankfully, it did not blow up."

Oxygen tents made from a canvas canopy, which covered the patient's upper torso, were used extensively during this time. The three-humidifier bottles, attached between the flow meter and the oxygen tank, needed frequent refilling with water. Deloris became adept at keeping the oxygen flowing into the tent and gained recognition as the "fixer" in demand by other nurses on the evening and night shifts.

Dorothy Ford Larson from St. Luke's Hospital School of Nursing in Kansas City, Missouri, remembered caring for a patient in an oxygen tent who had a blocked coronary artery. As with other heart patients confined to bed with no physical activity for 6 weeks, he was not allowed to feed himself.

Alone on the ward at 2:00 a.m., Dorothy attempted to crack the valve when oxygen swooshed out of the tank at an alarming rate. She said, "When this emergency arose, the patient got out of bed and helped me rectify the situation. I was sure one of us would die before morning. We both survived!"

"The three-bottle suction siphoning set-up, the Wangensteen, kept us hopping to make sure the device functioned properly," said Alice Noguchi Kanagaki from Madison General Hospital in Wisconsin. Cadet nurses attending the University of Minnesota remembered Dr. Owen Wangensteen, the famous surgeon who in the 1930s pioneered the suctioning method for conditions of the stomach, intestine, bladder, and lung cavities. When cadets saw a physician followed by a group of interns, they knew Dr. Wangensteen was on the ward.

In the 1940s a manufactured suction-apparatus was available, but Minneapolis General had no funding for new equipment. Cadet nurses improvised. Betty Deming Pearson said,

> When suction was ordered for our patients, we went to central supply for three jugs, corks with holes for glass tubing and several feet of rubber tubing. We arranged the bottles in a particular pattern filling the top bottle with water. Water flowed from the upper to the lower bottle creating the suction. Reversing the bottles to maintain the suction required strategic timing. A cadet nurse could only hope the supplies needed to assemble the suction apparatus would be available when ordered.

Albina Borho Reichmuth and other cadets could not understand why they found holes in the large soft stomach tubing. They later discovered the interns had confiscated the tubing for use as condoms.

Some cadet nurses became experts with the "Wangensteen," but others never overcame their fear and never understood the working principles of this formidable apparatus. Albina worked on call as surgical scrub nurse, assisting the surgeon in the sterile operating field with her friend assigned as circulating room nurse. The surgeon, in the middle of abdominal surgery with suctioning in progress, suddenly shouted, "Cut the suction!" Albina's friend took out her scissors and quickly cut the tubing. The surgeon, who meant for her to clamp the suction tubing, started screaming and throwing instruments. The cadet left the room in tears.

Cadet nurse Lucille North Vogt, attending the Los Angles County General Hospital School of Nursing found the operating room experience intriguing.

I remember the surgical staff lined up against the walls of the operating-room corridor as the head nurse bellowed out the day's surgical room assignments [for] scrub nurses-those who "scrubbed in" before donning rubber gloves to assist the surgeon in the sterile field; circulating nurses-those who carried out the tasks outside the sterile field. All others were to ... scrub the halls, walls, linen chutes, and hopper rooms. The hopper room derived its name from the receptacle for washing bloody linens and other contaminated objects.

With registered nurses unavailable, Lucille had the dubious pleasure of being the first student nurse to "scrub" for a brain surgery case with a renowned neurosurgeon. The surgeon declared, "We're signing this patient's death certificate by allowing a student to scrub on this case!"

While Lucille had more experience than many student nurses, she felt intimidated and scared. The surgeon picked up a saline bulb syringe used for irrigating, squirted her in the face and said, "How would you like that in your brain?"

"The saline was always too warm or too cool; nothing pleased him. However, the patient lived and did well."

In surgery, junior cadets memorized the names of instruments so they could quickly respond to the surgeon's request. Patricia Ruby Morse from the University of Minnesota said, "During [one] surgical procedure the surgeon yelled, 'Cripes!'" The assisting student cadet almost knocked over the sterile instrument tray looking for a "cripes."

Patricia said, " Our surgical orthopedic supervisor told us she should send us to the local trade school so we could learn the names of tools, such as hammer, chisel, saw, drill, etc."

Junior cadet nurse Shirley Morrison Francisco's favorite rotation at the Meadville City Hospital in Pennsylvania was the obstetrical department. Strategies to discourage stray germs included restricting visiting hours to adults for brief times in the afternoon and evenings and denying fathers admittance to the delivery room. Shirley remembered the new mothers who stayed in bed for up to 10 days with breasts and abdomens bound with straight pieces of cloth called binders. She said, "Our fingers bled from pushing safety pins, dull from frequent sterilizing, through the thick material to secure the binders that all new mothers wore."

The baby boom was on and cadet nurses often found hospital facilities inadequate. Claribel Carlson Crews remembered setting up a makeshift delivery room in the sunroom during a thunderstorm. The roof leaked and nurses and interns held pans over the soon-to-be mother in an effort to keep the field sterile.

Harriet McCann Kellogg from Robert Packer School of Nursing in Sayre, Pennsylvania, remembered how frightened she was in the labor room. "We were told that if an obstetrics patient "precipitated" in the labor room, we would be disgraced. I was convinced that if this happened to me I could never hold my head erect again!"

In the nursing vernacular of that time, a precipitate delivery was one that occurred in nonsterile surroundings with no physician present. Expectant mothers received narcotics for labor pains, producing sedation called twilight sleep. Precipitate births often occurred with little or no warning.

Ina Campbell Coulter from St. Elizabeth Hospital in Lincoln, Nebraska, recalled:

> My first day in obstetrics started off wrong. I was assigned to watch a woman under the influence of "twilight." The lady, a mother of several children, became restless and called out "The baby is here!" I lifted the bed sheet and sure enough, the baby had arrived. Seconds later the door opened and another nurse saw me looking terrified, holding the newborn baby by the feet. I confess I was never at [ease] on the maternity ward after that incident.

With little or no training, student nurses were expected to safely complete the delivery in the event of a precipitate birth. Our obstetrics textbook warned:

> When the birth emergency is over, the nurse becomes a tactful unassuming woman who is careful of the doctor's vanity and of the importance he should rightfully have in the eyes of the patient and the family. The good nurse never "stars"; she never plays to the "grandstand." She [the nurse] maintains a womanly wisdom which

woos the patient's and the family's confidence in the cooperative efforts of the medical surgical team (Woodard & Gardner, 1944, p. 729).

With one nurse to care for 30 babies in the Los Angeles County General Hospital, the newborn nursery was a challenging place to work. The routine for the babies included bathing, taking the temperatures, dressing the babies in shirts and diapers, wrapping them in blankets, placing the babies on the gurney, then taking them to the new mothers to feed. Some babies were bottle-fed dextrose and water. "I had no idea nursing would be this difficult," said Dorothie Melvin Crowley referring to Los Angeles County General Hospital.

Elaine Sandall Corona and June, her roommate, cared for 50 babies before going home to collapse. One night when June came back from a break, 50 bawling infants greeted her. She screamed, "SHUT UP!" A brief moment of silence followed, broken only by June's sobbing. A few weeks later June left the school of nursing to be married.

Nebraska's capital city had a large Army Air Corps base and many servicemen's wives had their babies at Lincoln General Hospital. Most Jewish women chose this non-sectarian hospital for the birth of their babies. "The Jewish circumcision ceremony, performed on the 8th day after birth by a Rabbi, took place in our hospital," Elaine said.

Because the extended families lived far away, they could not attend the circumcision celebration. The Rabbi, a refugee from Austria, knew that nurses changed shifts at 3:00 p.m. so he stood by the main elevator and invited the nurse cadets to "come and make a family!"

Cadet nurses signed the guest book and ate the Kosher food. With most food rationed and hard to obtain, we wondered how the Jewish family managed to serve such a sumptuous feast.

I also remembered [that] the assistant director of nursing attended, making sure we behaved properly and did not drink the wine!

Helen Harris Engle, a cadet at Tacoma General Hospital, remembered an interesting aspect of her maternity experience.

> Babies of illegitimate mothers were never on display. These young women, kept behind curtains, rarely had a visitor. They healed and quietly left the hospital without their babies. The cadets wanted to do more for them, but what? I was concerned because the wonderful happy moods and the sharing of "mama talk" in the maternity wards full of young mothers was noticeably absent among these shielded women.

A beautiful 23-year-old young woman cried out with pain one evening as she was wheeled onto a ward at Bellevue Hospital in New York City when Florence Berger Adler was on duty. The young woman had been pregnant, unmarried, and had gone to someone who had performed an abortion using a metal clothes hanger. Inadvertently her uterus was perforated. An overwhelming infection resulted and she died just 30 minutes after admission. Florence said, "This beautiful young woman succumbed as the result of the crude procedure. In 1946 having an illegitimate baby was a disgrace. In the process of hiding her shame, the young woman lost her life."

Caring for premature and low-birth-weight babies was difficult. Dorothy Luther said, "On the 11p.m. - 7 a.m. shift, two of us had total care of the three nurseries: one for black babies, one for white babies, and one for sick babies who needed isolation." Dorothy remembered one little preemie:

> He was placed in a separate room for close observation. His incubator consisted of a wooden box open at the top. A bare incandescent light bulb provided the heat source. The cadet nurses on duty took great care to keep his tiny body from touching the light bulb. We tried to stabilize his wildly fluctuating temperature by turning the light bulb on and off and by applying or removing his blanket. We weren't very successful with stabilization. The little fellow died.

Jacqueline Fickes Webster from Los Angeles County General Hospital School of Nursing thought the evening charge nurse on pediatrics was strange. Children with old bayonet wounds on their legs and clutching small bags given to them by the Red Cross arrived by ship from the prisoner-of-war camps. The charge nurse called these children her "pidgins" and spent a lot of her salary buying toys for them.

Jacqueline struggled to give her young charges their nose drops and set up croup tents. Then she too became smitten. There was a little brunette girl who was abandoned because she had a bilateral hip deformity and a little blonde boy no one wanted because he had hydrocephalus (water on the brain, as it was called). Jacqueline telephoned her mother regularly pleading, "PLEASE adopt these children."

Cadet nurse Charlotte Allen Rogers who attended the St. Mary's School of Nursing in Huntington, West Virginia, was impressed with what she saw regarding the care provided children with communicable diseases. A newborn baby was brought in with gonorrhea of the eyes. "We had no treatment except to wash the infant's eyes out with boric acid solution every 5 minutes 24 hours a day, and we did that for days. We saved the baby's eyes."

Anna Mable Mayer remembered how it felt when she lost her first infant patient while on the pediatric unit. "It was like experiencing a personal death. The baby had spina bifida, a congenital condition of the spine." Technology to save this baby was still decades away and Anna cared for the little one with fervor. The baby lingered for several days and when she died Anna carried her tiny body, wrapped in a blanket, to the morgue. She said, "That baby broke my heart."

Pediatrics was one of the most stressful assigned services for cadets with its congenital conditions, epidemic diseases, diarrhea, and infections taking a toll among infants and children. Remembering those times Ruth Ann Schultze Vogel, a cadet nurse from Nebraska, wrote the following poem.

AS ORDERED

"Prepare her," I thought. Tell her
"The surgeon will remove a plug from
the skull, like a watermelon,
to see if it is pink inside."

I told her, "The doctor wants me to
cut your hair. It will grow back."
Thinking, (to her, growing back will seem an eternity).

She saw my scissors and my tears.
She was very brave.
I parted her hair,
wove two thick braids,
tied and cut them, and
gave them to her to hold.

I cropped her hair close to the scalp,
shaved her head using lather,
a double edged razor and shaved again.
The whole process seemed to take forever.
Finally, it was finished.

She reached with both hands
clutching her bald head.
Courage gave way to sobbing.
We cried together.

In the a.m. I met the gurney in the hall.
She was being carted off to surgery.
She never returned.
Diagnosis: TB of the brain
And I-
I write that I might wash away the pain.

The cadet nurses, in their teens, often alone on the wards, inexperienced and untrained in dealing with a family's grief, and with their own grief when a youngster died, accumulated lifelong remembrances of difficult times.

References

Goostray, S. (1943, October). Problems with cadet nurse school curriculum: Glamour not enough-the job is to educate. **Hospitals,** pp. 65-67.

Keefer, C.S. (1943). Penicillin. **American Journal of Nursing, 43(12),** 1076-1077.

Laws authorizing nurse training program: Payments to provide training for nurses (Chap. 126). Pub. L.74, 78th Cong. 1st Sess. (1943).

McConnell, J.P. (1942). Volunteer nurses aides. **American Journal of Nursing, 42(5),** 506-507.

Woodard, H.L., & Gardner, B. (1944). Obstetrical management and nursing. (p. 729). Philadelphia, PA: Davis.

11

Good-Bye Home Hospital
by Thelma M. Robinson

Two hours before train time, our director of nurses called a small group of cadet nurses into her office and seated us in a semi-circle around her desk. She cleared her throat and said,

> You are about to embark on a new experience, a 3-month affiliation in psychiatric nursing. Some of you will enjoy this time and want to make this area of nursing your life work. All will return with greater knowledge, skills, and understanding of mental illness, and you will be better nurses for it.
>
> Although you are out of range of my watchful eye, I expect you to maintain the high nursing standards that we set at Lincoln General Hospital School of Nursing. Please conduct yourselves in a manner that will bring respect to the nurses of our hospital. You can expect a visit from me almost anytime. I plan to check on how you are doing.

Back in the nurses' residence we scurried with the last bit of packing. A clatter sounded through the halls as we carried the boxes of books and other items we would not need for the next 3 months to the attic. Already classmates from the lower grades were moving into our vacated rooms. Cadet nurses on night duty trying to sleep yelled, "Quiet!"

We were excited as we put on our cadet nurse uniforms and checked each other's stockings to make sure the seams were straight. Wearing our uniforms assured us "special travel rates." The train ride took us to Ingleside, the state mental hospital in south central Nebraska. Old and newer hospital buildings, a post office and general store, a bakery, and a butcher shop were clustered around a gazebo bandstand. A large farm surrounding the grounds provided work opportunities for patients and supplied most of the food for Ingleside residents.

We were housed in a new brick apartment complex with no housemother and we reveled in our new freedom. We were assigned to a team comprised of students from other schools of nursing and enjoyed comparing experiences with other cadet nurses. A naval ammunition depot at nearby Hastings, Nebraska, provided sailors and dancing on Saturday nights.

The U.S. Cadet Nurse Corps encouraged schools of nursing to offer cadet nurses affiliations beyond what was available at their home hospitals. This provided broader clinical opportunities for cadets and also provided service to other hospitals or agencies. In addition affiliations produced increased enrollment in schools of nursing, which furthered the national recruitment goal of doubling the number of nurse students above that of normal times. Also, with nursing expanding to a larger community, more citizens could benefit from better health care (Petry & Spalding, 1943).

A 1945 study conducted by the USPHS showed that 48% of the schools of nursing offered an experience in psychiatric nursing. An additional 11% of the schools offered the experience only to some students (Faveau, 1945). This report stated that the extension in this specialized field (psychiatry) was in harmony with the plans for the provision of a more complete health program for the country in the post-World War II years.

In their psychiatric affiliations, cadet nurses experienced a different kind of nursing. Elaine Sandall Corona from Lincoln General Hospital in Nebraska remembered her first day at Ingleside.

My classmate, Bernie, and I reported at 7:00 a.m. to the Women's Receiving Ward, a locked ward. The night nurse, who had been on duty for 16 hours straight, handed us the keys and promptly walked off the ward. We didn't know what to do, so I called the nursing director. The nurse in charge said she was sorry but we were on our own and advised us to do the best we could.

Hospital workers observed the patients from the glassed-in nurses' station so we read the shift reports and reviewed the patients' charts. Together we ventured outside the secured area and greeted the patients. Two women who lived permanently on the ward sidled up and told us what to do next.

We managed to muddle through the day except for one problem. Every hour a little man knocked on the door and asked for the keys. Each time we refused. Late in the day one of the women informed us that all he wanted to do was to clean the office. We gave him the keys and he cleaned and we were all happy.

Cadet nurses attended classes in psychiatry. Elaine remembered one young professor, a refugee from Vienna, who had temporary credentials. She was pleased to learn the Austrian professor followed the Jungian school of psychology because she was not an advocate of Freudian theory. "His lectures included [advice about] how to make our future marriages work," she said.

Gail Churchill Sorensen affiliated at the Rochester State Psychiatric Hospital in New York where Mrs. Bullard, the superintendent of nurses, oriented her class of cadet nurses with some interesting facts. Thirty-seven cents a day fed, housed, and provided care for one patient. Patients who were able to do so worked in the kitchen, on the farm that produced much of the food, and elsewhere in the institution while coping with their mental illnesses. Supplies and adequate facilities were often lacking. One ward had only one bathtub and two combs for 80 patients. Scabies was prevalent on the ward that housed the elderly.

One of Gail's instructors taught the cadets about mental illness stating mental illness was not a disease of weird, abnormal people but that everyone had a breaking point and sometimes just a fine line existed between normal and abnormal behavior. Cadets learned the ways of clever, charming sociopaths and learned about the mood swings and flight of ideas of manic-depressives. They gained an understanding of obsessive behavior and the three kinds of schizophrenics defined at that time: simple (those who withdrew and stayed in their rooms living in their own worlds), hebephrenic (those who acted foolish and laughed a lot), and catatonic (those who sat or stood like statues). Cadet nurses rotated frequently in order to experience the different types of mental illness and the therapies in use during the '40s.

One Nebraska cadet nurse from St. Elizabeth Hospital School of Nursing remembered ward 21, a large women's unit. This ward housed the most serious mentally ill patients who were in straitjackets. The sounds of incoherent jabbering often met cadet nurses when they unlocked the door of the ward to begin work. Then the odor of feces and urine hit their nostrils as they entered the ward. Ina Campbell Coulter described it this way, "The nurse who worked this ward was given top priority for the shower as soon as she got off duty. Her clothes were quickly tossed outside the door before the aroma from her clothes permeated the entire apartment."

Off-duty student nurses were expected to attend the Friday afternoon dances for patients at Ingleside. Elaine Sandall Corona and the other cadets entered the social hall to find the men patients lined up on one side and the women on the other. The social director stood at a table with a phonograph and directed the cadets to intermingle with the women patients. The music started and the men headed for the small band of nurse students. For the first time in her life, Elaine wished she were a wallflower. The cadets tried to get the men patients to dance with the women patients, but they would not comply.

Some wards at Ingleside experimented with color as therapy; bedside units were painted green, blue, rose, and lavender. A continuous bath, used as a sedative, was another kind of therapy that was used to calm disturbed patients. Cadets would wrap patients in muslin bandages, place them on a hammock with the head resting on a rubber cushion and lower them into tepid water. Cadets happily tried this soothing and relaxing treatment. They also tried on straitjackets to get the feel of restriction. But they refused to try shock therapy. According to Anne Higgins Murphy:

> We did not volunteer to serve as a patient for the shock treatments. Both electric and insulin shock treatments were given at this time. Prior to the procedure we would boil potatoes in water and make a thick slurry. After the insulin shock procedure, we gave the patients the potato water to speed [their blood-sugar levels] back to normal. When we missed breakfast, we drank [some] ourselves.

Electric shock treatment was an effective but dangerous treatment at that time. One cadet, who was assisting with the treatment, saw a patient develop respiratory distress following an injection of curare, a muscle relaxant usually given before the shock treatment. Desperate attempts including artificial respiration failed to revive him. The patient died.

After caring for hundreds of patients, cadet nurses rejoiced when occasionally a mentally ill patient became well enough to go home. And thanks to the cadets, psychiatric patients were more adequately cared for during the late war and post-war years than they probably would have been otherwise. Mental health workers had left by the hundreds for bigger paychecks with war industries. The few remaining mental health workers were often untrained. "The patients enjoyed having us rather than the aides; we were sympathetic, kind, and creative in meeting their needs," said Elaine Sandall Corona.

When hospital schools of nursing proliferated after World War I, the content and scope of student nurse clinical experiences were often limited to the opportunities available in the particular hospital offering a nurse training program. However, when the country's poverty and communicable disease problems increased during the '30s, the nurses' role expanded to include the community. As a consequence of these changes in nurses' roles, leaders at progressive schools of nursing began to offer affiliations for additional clinical experiences in public health nursing and communicable disease (Carrington, 1940).

Anne Higgins Murphy explained it this way:

> Affiliations with agencies away from our home hospital were exciting and added greatly to our growth. While on the contagious disease affiliation at Kingston Avenue Hospital in Brooklyn for 3 months I used the "magic rag," a wash cloth in a basin of alcohol. With it wound around my hand, I wiped contaminated objects that could not be autoclaved (sterilized with steam under pressure). Those basins were everywhere.

Medicated steam was the treatment of choice for patients with diphtheria and croup (Harmer & Henderson, 1939). Cadets made croup tents by draping a sheet on a frame that fit over the bed. A croup kettle with a long spout required the nurses' vigilance to make sure the patient was in a position to derive the most benefit from the steam and at the same time be protected from being scalded or burned. Anne recalled the croup rooms at Kingston Hospital, an innovation for that time. These special rooms equipped with steam outlets gave relief to children with croup or diphtheria as well as to the nurses who could assure greater safety for their patients.

Anne Higgins Murphy also affiliated with the Visiting Nurse Service on Henry Street and cared for families living in poverty in New York City tenements. As a cadet nurse from the prestigious Flower-Fifth Avenue Hospital School of Nursing in New York City, Anne remembered feeling horrified at seeing a baby's face that had been nibbled by a rat searching for milk.

Students from Madison General Hospital School of Nursing had the privilege of affiliating at Cook County Hospital in Chicago, a foremost teaching hospital in the nation at that time. "Cook County provided additional learning experiences in psychiatry, neurology, and pediatrics," Alice Noguchi Kanagaki said. "We met girls from the East Coast, Texas, and North Dakota, as well as from schools of nursing all over the Midwest."

Barbara Oetzel Lenthart, said:

For a naïve girl from a small Wisconsin town, Cook County Hospital was a cultural shock beyond description. While there I discovered cockroaches the size of mice. While working in the pediatric ward, I came on duty to discover the exterminator had earlier spread roach powder in the ward. My patients were armed with paper towels rolled for swatting. Not familiar with these insects, I found their abundance disturbing. I looked down, saw one on my uniform and shrieked in terror. A young patient said, "Oh nursey, they won't hurt you. Help us swat!" We had a wonderful time swatting.

With communicable diseases-especially tuberculosis-rampant, Margaret Cromheecke Ammerman cared for acutely ill children at the Glen Lake Tuberculosis Sanitarium in Minnesota. She recalled, "Each afternoon we covered the children with blankets and raised the windows for their fresh air treatment. What a joy to note the slightest improvement in just one young patient's condition.

Norma Booth Krats from the University of Minnesota School of Nursing also affiliated at Glen Lake. "The food was wonderful, the setting beautiful. The coughing patients wore masks but we weren't allowed this protection," Norma said.

The incidence of illness and death from tuberculosis for young women peaked in the early '40s. Because of exposure and fatigue, student nurses were at greater risk than the average population. The National League for Nursing collected information that showed 75% to 100% of the student nurses from schools of nursing associated with large hospitals would acquire a positive tuberculin reaction during their training (Riggins & Amberson, 1940).

Venereal disease treatment for some patients meant suffering from two diseases. Gail Churchill Sorenson described one of her patients.

He was a nice man in his 40s having a flare-up of syphilis. He told me that 20 years prior he had made a foolish mistake.

The patient's doctor injected him with malaria, the theory being that periodic fevers over 105° might kill the syphilis spirochete. I remember the doctor saying, "Maybe we can cure one disease with another and we know we can cure malaria."

Ruth Ann Schultze Vogel remembered meticulously carrying out isolation techniques as she cared for patients with diphtheria, meningitis, scarlet fever, measles, and whooping cough at Douglas County Hospital in Omaha, Nebraska.

> A mother and her three children were ill with diphtheria. The father of this family raised a ladder to the second story window and helped them escape. They were out on the street to infect more of the community before we had a chance to prevent their leaving.

On the 17th anniversary of public health nursing, in March 1947 Corps Director Lucile Petry sent a memo to cadet nurses:

> If you like to teach individuals as well as groups, if you like to be outdoors in all kinds of weather, if you like the challenge of working with improvised equipment in the home, if you can sense the drama in the prevention of illness, you should consider public health nursing in planning your future (Petry, 1947, p. 4).

Cincinnati General Hospital, a 1,100-bed hospital, offered clinical experiences in all areas except visiting nursing, a service that took place in the community. For their public health experience Janet Schramm Abernathy and other cadets accompanied a Visiting Nurse Association (VNA) staff nurse through the more affluent part of town, then spent the rest of their 3-month affiliation working in the Cincinnati ghettos. Their blue VNA uniforms and black bags gave them identity, which made them feel safe when visiting run-down apartment buildings and miserable little cottages. "I remember changing a dressing by the only light available, a kerosene lamp, and trying to teach diabetics who lived in dirt-ridden homes to give their own insulin injections," said Janet.

Virginia Bogan Charnock was a cadet nurse at the Sisters of Charity Hospital School of Nursing in Buffalo, New York. For her public health clinical experience she received an assignment to a section of the city including the ghetto.

She said, "I was filled with fear but the families accepted me into their community with open arms and respect."

Stella Goostray, president of the National League for Nursing, said:

> We are asking 65,000 young women to enter our schools at a time when the world is theirs. Neither the glamour of the uniform, nor the attraction of all expenses paid, not the jingle of money in the change purse, nor the appeal to patriotic motives is going to attract the kind of young women we want in our schools. They can get all of these in other branches of the service ... these young women will have to be assured that in a nursing school they are getting something more, and that "something more" is a sound preparation for a career (Goostray, 1943, pp. 65-67).

Remembering World War II and the postwar years, the cadets agreed the Corps indeed gave them "something more" through the opportunity of affiliations. Dorothie Melvin Crowley said it well:

> My cadet experience challenged me intellectually and physically. I learned about myself and what I was capable of doing. I look back on those years with great nostalgia and with pride that I made it! History and circumstances came together in the right way, at the right time, to offer me right life choices.

References

Carrington, M. (1940). Affiliations for student nurse, factors which the home school must consider. **American Journal of Nursing, 40**(3), 298-300.

Faveau, C.H. (1945). **Opportunities in psychiatric nursing.** (USPHS Report No. 2664, 1233-7). (RG 90). Washington, DC: National Archives and Records Administration.

Goostray, S. (1943, October). Problems of cadet nurse school curriculum, glamour not enough-the job is to educate. **Hospitals,** 65-67.

Harmer, B., & Henderson, V. (1939). The principles and practice of nursing (4th ed., p. 562). New York: Macmillan.

Petry, L. (1947). Memo to you. **Cadet Nurse Corps News, 2,** p. 4. (Cadet Nurse File). Bethesda, MD: National Library of Medicine.

Petry, L., & Spalding, E.K. (1943). The production front in nursing. **American Journal of Nursing, 43**(10), 900-901.

Riggins, H.M., & Amberson, J.B. (1940). The detection and control of tuberculosis among nurses. **American Journal of Nursing, 40**(10), 1137-1146.

12

War On The Home Front—Polio
by Thelma M. Robinson

Cadet nurses helped fight another war, the escalating war against poliomyelitis. At the turn of the century this disease, known as infantile paralysis, generally associated with dirt and poverty, rarely attacked adults. The public changed its perception of the malady when a wealthy young man was struck, a man who would never walk on his own again. That man became president of the United States, Franklin Delano Roosevelt (Rogers, 1992).

My first experience with polio care was similar to that of other cadets. On the door was a sign with bold letters, ISOLATION—NO ADMISSION. I put the isolation gown over my student uniform, tied the strings of my facemask, and entered the polio ward at Lincoln General Hospital. All the hospital rooms were full and the corridor was jammed with beds and cribs, some with patients in them. A respirator, called an iron lung, was vacant and available for the next polio victim.

The nurse in charge had recently received training at the Kenny Institute in Minneapolis and taught the cadets how to prepare and apply hot packs according to the Kenny Method. The Kenny packs were made from old woolen blankets cut into pieces to fit each part of the body.

We worked in teams of two and began by filling a tub with scalding hot water and placing the pieces of wool in the water. While one person cranked the hand wringer, the second person, using tongs, lifted the pieces of dripping, steaming wool from the hot water and fed them through the rollers. Packs were wrung twice to remove as much water as possible so that patients would not be burned. We placed the Kenny packs in rubber sheets to maintain the heat and carried them to the patients' bedsides.

We worked quickly and gently as we removed the cold set of packs from the patients and applied the steaming set. We covered each affected muscle with hot wool packs topped with rubber sheeting. Sometimes a patient would be swathed from neck to toes except for the joints. Use of the Kenny method called for leaving joints exposed so that patients would be free to move as tolerated. The packs were applied around the clock until the patients' painful muscle spasms subsided. The grim siege of pain could last anywhere from 2 weeks to several months. When the painful stage passed, patients relearned to use their muscles (Stevenson, 1942). Patients treated by the Kenny method were ready for rehabilitative therapy sooner than were those who had the usual medical treatment of immobilization (Daly, Greenbaum, Reilly, Weiss, & Stimson, 1942).

Cadets did not complain about the hot and heavy work and patients looked forward to receiving their packs and rested comfortably without pain medication. One patient on the ward had a private-duty nurse. His attending physician was a prominent orthopedic surgeon who held to the belief that immobilization was the treatment of choice. His patient, who was immobilized in a plaster cast, needed narcotics periodically for the terrible pain.

Although the treatment was revolutionary, use of the Kenny method was handicapped by the fact that a nurse developed this treatment for polio. In 1949 the press accosted Sister Kenny on her first visit to the United States as she disembarked from the ship in San Francisco. Her fame as the polio messiah from Australia became well known, but the medical community throughout the country remained skeptical (Miller, 1944). Sister Kenny, a strong-minded person, treaded on sensitive toes. In

Denver she saw polio patients in splints and casts and called them "plastic prisoners." In New York City Sister Kenny presented her letter of introduction to the National Foundation for Infantile Paralysis. She received a polite brush-off.

Big and strong looking, Sister Kenny stared at physicians in Chicago with piercing eyes and talked with an air of authority about the symptoms and treatment of polio. Some physicians said it would be difficult to work with this unsophisticated lady who always appeared in a shapeless black outfit and large brimmed hat (Cohn, 1975).

Discouraged, Sister Kenny made one last stop at the Mayo Clinic in Rochester, Minnesota, before heading home to Australia. Here a physician suggested that she visit the Minneapolis/St. Paul area where an epidemic 8 months earlier had left victims aching and emaciated, strapped and immobilized with frames, splints, and casts. There in the Twin Cities, a few physicians began to listen, realizing the Australian reports regarding Sister Kenny were positive.

One physician from Minneapolis allowed her to treat a young man who had contracted polio during a recent epidemic. The physician had initially followed the traditional restraining treatment and immobilized the affected leg and shoulder. Kenny's rehabilitation began by removing the splints and applying hot packs until the spasms abated. She then began passive exercises by gently moving the young man's arms and legs. She told him to think about the movement and to talk to his affected muscles and make them work. By the first snowfall, the young man was shoveling snow. His physician then removed the frames, splints, and casts from all of his polio patients (Cohn, 1975).

Word spread and a few physicians decided that further investigation was necessary. "What do you need to stay?" they asked Sister Kenny. "A bed and a meal a day," she replied (Cohn, 1975).

The March of Dimes provided the funds for her maintenance. Still many physicians remained dubious, including a young orthopedic specialist, Dr. John Pohl. He had obtained his education at Harvard University and Boston Children's Hospital, where strict immobilization for polio patients was emphasized. Although skeptical of Kenny and her methods, he was tired of hearing the cries of his polio patients in casts. He asked Sister Kenny to treat one of his patients. She did and he marveled at the results. Dr. John Pohl became a Kenny convert.

Dr. Pohl, heading the Minneapolis General Hospital Infantile Paralysis Clinic, asked the board for additional space and equipment. When the season's first polio patient arrived in August, the Kenny clinic was ready. That year only a few polio patients were admitted, but they were all that Sister Kenny and her assistant could handle. Dr. Pohl recorded the progress of each polio patient and wrote an article advocating the Kenny treatment for poliomyelitis (Pohl, 1942).

But many physicians still preferred other treatments. In June 1944, in the midst of the worst polio outbreak in 25 years, orthopedic surgeons met in Chicago for an American Medical Association conference. A committee reported the Kenny treatment for infantile paralysis had questionable value and charged that the public and many members of the medical community had been misled (Ghormley et al., 1944). On the other hand, the medical profession recognized the need to reevaluate the treatment of poliomyelitis and to treat the disease more effectively.

Sister Kenny remained in the United States for 7 years teaching her polio techniques and crusading for polio patients. Many cadet nurses who had been enrolled in schools of nursing in Minnesota and Michigan worked with Sister Kenny. Camilla Ecklund Johnson said:

> She was an imposing figure with short, straight hair. She always wore black cotton stockings. Rumor had it that the thick stockings were to cover old shrapnel scars on her legs from World War I. I was impressed with her stature, friendliness, and teaching techniques.

The rumor was true. Sister Kenny had served with a British Red Cross unit in France and Belgium during World War I. A shell tore through the ward, striking her in the leg. Her long painful recovery and her determination to walk again inspired her polio patients. The Australians called their nurses "Sister," the title Sister Kenny kept throughout her career (Cohn, 1975).

Betty Deming Pearson remembered the day when 100 patients with symptoms of polio were admitted to Minneapolis General Hospital; 145 diagnostic spinal taps were done on these and other patients. Triage techniques were used to separate those needing iron lungs from those to receive the Kenny packs. The hospital was filled to capacity as more patients continued to come.

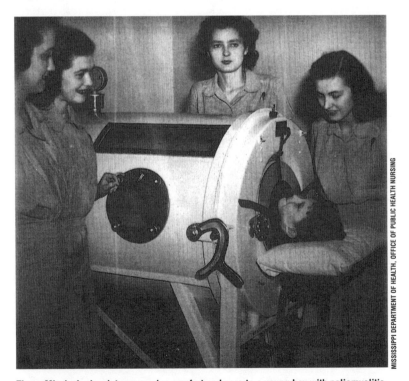

These Mississippi cadet nurses give comfort and care to a young boy with poliomyelitis. The "iron lung" was used to help the child's breathing. Three Mississippi schools of nursing participated in the U.S. Cadet Nurse Corps program—those at the Mississippi Baptist Hospital, Vicksburg Hospital, and Biloxi Hospital.

On the banks of the Mississippi was a school for "crippled" children with all the needed equipment for a hospital except beds. Desks were replaced with beds and the school became a makeshift hospital, which was soon filled with children recently diagnosed with polio. Cadet nurse Betty Pearson was assigned to work there for the remainder of her diet kitchen experience.

Betty and the other cadets rode out to the school in an old ambulance, leaving at 6:00 a.m. and returning at 7:00 p.m. For their dietary activities they passed food trays, fed patients who needed help, and passed juice twice a day. But they spent most of their time passing medications, giving baths, and helping with the Kenny packs.

Visitors were not allowed so many parents volunteered to help in order to be with their children. Once they saw the effectiveness of the hot packs, the parents recruited others. "We had wonderful volunteer help," Betty said.

Sister Kenny visited the school frequently. Betty's job was to offer her juice and detain her a bit to give the nurses time to prepare for her visit. Sister Kenny's eagle eyes saw many details and they had to be right.

Another cadet had this experience. While on night duty, Helen Ten Brink Wyngarden at Butterworth Hospital in Michigan attended a young woman encapsulated in an iron lung with only her head exposed. One night in a distressed, whispered voice, the patient asked, "Why did this happen to me?" Helen felt as though she were on trial. She hoped for insight, patted her patient's face, and said,

> [Cora], when you were home caring for your husband and three little girls, with your family around, busy with your home and garden, did you ever ask, "Why did this happen to me?"

> Months later after iron lung [life support], Kenny packs, muscle retraining, and a young mother's determination, doctors reported, "By the grace of God and [Cora's] pluck, she's walking!"

Camilla Ecklund Johnson from the University of Minnesota School of Nursing had a harrowing experience she will never forget. Sister Kenny did not like iron lungs but sometimes the clumsy respirators gave polio patients the needed time to heal. Patients trapped in iron lungs and their nurses feared the power outages that occurred frequently during violent summer storms. Camilla remembered a time when the hospital's power went off. She grabbed the handle and manually pumped the iron lung before the auxiliary power came on. She said, "It was strenuous and frightening knowing that the patient's life depended on me."

Cadet nurses who worked the night shifts during polio epidemics will always remember the eerie rhythmic swish, wheeze, and thump of the iron lungs. Often more iron lungs were in operation than there were nurses to operate the manual pump in the event of a power outage. On those nights cadet nurses caring for their polio patients prayed for clear skies.

Mary Black Bergland, also from the University of Minnesota School of Nursing, recalled her feelings one early morning when she cared for three patients and watched each die of the dreaded bulbar polio. This type of polio paralyzed respiratory and swallowing muscles. Mary said, "I wondered when the scene would end. Would it take us all?"

Cadet nurse Cynthia Clark Crocker became ill while on affiliation at the state mental hospital. When she returned to her home hospital school of nursing in Bangor, Maine, they gave her many tests. After several consultations, Cynthia was diagnosed as having polio, and she was moved to an isolation ward where she received the Kenny treatment. She recovered with only slight muscle weakness but missed 6 weeks of training and had to make up that time before she could graduate.

Ex-cadet nurse Polly Jean Felton was a patient at Warm Springs, Georgia, recovering from infantile paralysis. She was proud to have sung the solo hymn at the church service that President Roosevelt attended in early April 1945 ("Cadet Nurse," 1945). As a member of the minstrel troupe, which had scheduled a special performance for the president, she was ready in costume and grease paint ... but just a few minutes before curtain time the actors learned that President Roosevelt was dead. Polly Jean said, "It was a day and a time we will never forget. We loved him deeply."

The last cadet nurse graduating class of Lincoln General Hospital School of Nursing in Nebraska became concerned when their classmate, Betty Almquist, contracted polio. When her respiratory muscles failed she was placed in an iron lung. With 3 years of nurses' training winding down, senior cadet nurses served that summer as assistant head nurses or wherever the hospital needed them the most. After work they crammed for state boards, the exam they had to pass to become registered nurses. Despite their busy schedules, Betty's friends volunteered during their time off to be her special nurse.

In early fall of 1948, her classmates gathered at the state house along with other graduating nurses from throughout the state to take the grueling 2-day examination. Their instructor came to be a proctor. She told the class that Betty had died early that morning. Numb and shocked, the senior cadets filed into Nebraska's Unicameral Chamber to take the state board examination. Later, at the funeral service Betty lay in her coffin wearing the coveted all-while graduate nurse uniform, her first and only time.

Over these indelible memories of bright, young children crippled for life in the random lottery of polio, is the marvelous sequel of the many who were spared. In the late '50s former cadet nurse Helen Marie Harris Engle from Tacoma, Washington took her three little boys to the school nurse's room where they were given free polio immunizations. The school nurse used an eyedropper to drip a clear liquid onto sugar cubes. Marie said:

> As I watched my children swallow those sugar cubes, I wept with joy at the miracle of the moment.
>
> Having the fear of polio lifted from me and millions of other mothers like me was the event of the century. We were living in a new era.

References

Cadet nurse was soloist at last church services late president attended. (1945, July). **Cadet nurse corps news,** 1, p. 3. (Cadet Nurse File). Bethesda, MD: National Library of Medicine.

Cohn, V. (1975). **Sister Kenny: The woman who challenged the doctors.** (pp. 55; 126-133). Minneapolis, MN: The University Press.

Daly, M.I., Greenbaum, J., Reilly, E.T., Weiss, A. M., & Stimson, P.M. (1942). The early treatment of poliomyelitis with an evaluation of Sister Kenny treatment. **JAMA,** 118(17), 1433-1436.

Ghormley, R.K., Compere, E.L., Dickson, J.A., Funsten, R.V., Key, J.A., McCarroll, H.R., & Schumm, H.C. (1944). Evaluation of the Kenny treatment of infantile paralysis. **JAMA,** 125(7), 466-469.

Miller, L.M. (1944, October). Sister Kenny vs. the medical old guard. **Reader's Digest,** pp. 65-71.

Pohl, J.P. (1942). The Kenny treatment of anterior poliomyelitis (infantile paralysis) report of the first cases treated in America. **JAMA,** 118(17), 1428-1433.

Rogers, N. (1992). **Dirt and disease polio before FDR** (pp. 165-171). New Brunswick, NJ: Rutgers University Press.

Stevenson, J. (1942). The Kenny method: Nursing responsibilities in relation to the Kenny method of treatment of infantile paralysis. **American Journal of Nursing, 42,** 904-909.

13

Rules and Relationships
by Thelma M. Robinson

In the '40s the hospital schools of nursing, steeped in military, monastic, and medical traditions, outnumbered collegiate schools of nursing, 10 to one. The predominant educational system for nurses at that time involved training within the hospital setting. Young women attended classes, but 80% of their time was spent providing ward service over the 3-year period in the hospital where they trained (Kalisch & Kalisch, 1975).

Schools of nursing imposed rules and regulations as well as protocols for working relationships in order to maintain discipline and to protect and preserve their labor force. Student nurses were expected to be respectful, obedient, cheerful, dedicated, and submissive to authority and at the same time be caring, attentive, and skillful in the care of their patients. Did the cadet nurses ever break the rules? Here are some stories told by the cadets themselves. One said:

> You darn betcha! I had a bike, and I slipped out of the nurses' home at night to get 5-cent hamburgers. I went to the dorm basement as if to get clothes off the line, grabbed my bike, then pedaled through the tunnel to St. Joseph Hospital and off to the hamburger joint in Alliance, Nebraska. I was not apprehended; the nurses on duty wanted hamburgers, too. They let me in and out (Edna Coulter Schruben).

Another infraction of the rules was doing the laundry during study hour. However, Delores Giltner who attended Seton

School of Nursing in Colorado Springs found absolution for the error with her quick thinking. When the housemother confronted Delores, she feigned surprise at what day of the week it was. The housemother excused her. Delores also confessed to propping open the tunnel door that led to the hospital so that those who stayed out beyond curfew could get into the nurses' residence. The night supervisor had the only key to the tunnel door. She reported all the students for whom she unlocked the door and they received some form of punishment. No one suspected Delores of being an accessory to "crime"; she was never caught.

Stealing food from the hospital, then eating in one's room was a common offense. A cadet's flowing cape often concealed food smuggled into the nurses' residence for students and their insatiable appetites. Delores remembered a classmate who brought fruit juice and cake from the dietary kitchen on a regular basis and threw parties. One evening she brought a gorgeous cake to the nurses' residence. Leisurely, the cadet nurses began to eat the special delight. Then another classmate came off duty and reported that a great commotion was going on back at the hospital; a cake that was baked for a nun's birthday had disappeared. Delores said, "We ate cake so fast we were nearly sick."

The cadets threw the cardboard cake box down the incinerator chute just before inspection. Nothing was discovered and the parties continued.

Mary Tamplen Rupel deliberately broke a rule as a junior cadet at Lubbock General Hospital. Her parents lived 165 miles away and she saw them only once a year. Her mother had the opportunity to visit and although it was against the rules for her to visit in Mary's room, the cadets arranged for her stay overnight there with Mary. Mary's roommates helped smuggle dinner and breakfast from the hospital for her mother.

Mary even served her sequestered mother a special treat. She said:

We had a chef named Charles, a gourmet cook by today's definition. I can still taste his Boston cream pie. Charles left extra goodies on the dumb-waiter for the night nurses, the Boston cream pie being one of his specialties, which we shared with mother.

Parents were allowed a brief visit to their daughters' rooms only around the time of the capping celebration. Mary said, "The housemother apparently was unaware of mother's stay and did not confront me. Happy to see my mother, I was willing to suffer the consequences."

Ruby Hudgins Johns attended Akron City Hospital in Ohio and remembered her senior cadet days when she lived on the fifth floor of the dorm. One night after "lights out," she and her roommate invited classmates to their room to listen to "romantic music" on the phonograph. One of the records was Wayne King's husky-throated rendition of "Melody of Love" with his orchestra's dreamy musical background. Seated on the floor in darkness the cadets swooned and the housemother demanded to be let in. She said, "Open this door immediately! I know you have a man in there. I heard him talking. You know it's against the rules. OPEN UP THIS MINUTE!"

Struggling to stifle their giggles, the cadets scrambled under the beds and into the closets, except for Ruby and her roommate. Ruby opened the door, turned on the lights, played the record for the housemother, and apologized profusely for causing the disturbance. The housemother, nicknamed "Mousey" by the students, bought the story. Ruby said, "Thank goodness she didn't look under the beds. If she found the other girls, we'd all have been 'campused.'" To be campused meant being restricted to the nurses' residence and was a common method for punishing students who broke the rules.

New nursing students often studied the rules to try to avoid an infraction. Some examples of the rules were that at 8:00 p.m. a bell rang that meant first year students were confined to their rooms for study. At 9:30 p.m. a gong sounded and students had one-half hour to head for the shower, get a last cigarette smoke, or stand in line for the telephone. At 10:00 p.m. the housemother made rounds to assure everyone was in her room.

Provided a cadet was not scheduled for work, she could have one late leave until midnight each weekend. Once a month, on receipt of a letter mailed by a parent or guardian, the director of nursing granted permission for a student to spend the night away from the nurses' residence. The director of a school of nursing during this time explained, "I know my rules were tough! They had to be. Thousands of second lieutenants at the air base, interested in my pretty students, were a worry."

Being energetic and rebellious by nature, Alice Noguchi Kanagaki, who attended Madison General Hospital School of Nursing in Wisconsin, found it difficult to abide by the rules. While others avoided detection, she got caught. She said:

> One time I was invited to a classmate's home for the weekend. There wasn't time to get a written permission from my parents, so I forged one. The biggest blizzard in the history of the Midwest hit that weekend. The roads closed and all forms of transportation ceased to move. I notified the school of my dilemma and disclosed my crime. I was campused for a month and missed my brother's wedding.

It was nearly impossible for cadet nurses to get through 3 years of stringent regulations without breaking some rule. Some cadets did better than others. Virginia Forcier Scattarelli carried a small statue of St. Jude (the patron saint of hopeless cases) in her uniform pocket to help her avoid breaking rules.

The sisters at the College of Saint Catherine in Minnesota were stern and strict. For instance, a booth pay phone on the third floor of the nurses' residence could only be used during limited hours. *Open the Door Richard* was a popular song at the time, so a cadet friend of Virginia's took a cartoon that mentioned the song and changed the words to read *Open the Door Sister* and taped it to the booth. Her friend was campused.

While attending Mercy Hospital School of Nursing in Ohio, curiosity caused trouble for Dolores Gast Struewing. A large bell with a rope attached hung at the entrance of the hospital. She inquired several times about the purpose of the bell, but no one gave her a satisfying answer. Dolores decided to find out first-hand so she pulled ever so gently on the rope. A deafening sound followed. Terrified she ran to the nearby stairs and found herself face to face with the director of nursing, an unsmiling Sister of size.

The Sister ushered the shaking Virginia to her office and asked her to explain her actions. A long pause followed. Then Virginia squeaked out that she just wanted to know what the bell was for. The Sister calmly asked if she had found the answer. Virginia said "I think it is there to awaken the dead." The Sister's stern face broke into a grin and she said. "If God would will it, we would use it for that purpose. However the bell is there to notify people of a fire."

At the age of four, after her mother died, Barbara Edwards Benjamin lived with her grandparents in Pennsylvania. Barbara's grandmother was determined Barbara would get an education but had no idea where the money for it would come from. The U.S. Cadet Nurse Corps provided the opportunity. For Barbara, breaking a rule was not even considered. "I would not do anything to jeopardize my career by breaking a rule. It meant too much to Grandmother and me. I was the first one in my family to get a higher education.

Charrie Gerling Blake coped well with rules and regulations at Highland Hospital School of Nursing in New York until she went to the affiliated private tuberculosis hospital. Charrie and her friends enjoyed dancing at a local nickelodeon place. Having a roaring good time one night, they ignored curfew and were caught coming in late. When Charrie returned to her home school of nursing, she had to go before the board of nurses where she received a 5-day suspension. All lost time had to be made up after graduation before the young women could receive their diplomas, so after her classmates left following graduation Charrie had to remain to make up the 5 days.

Upon entry to the Robert Packer School of Nursing in Pennsylvania, Beryl Boardman Cleary and other new cadets signed a contract that they would "happily" abide by the rules. Still it was difficult not to break a rule because there were so many. After being ill with pneumonia and complications of a lung abscess during her training days, Beryl found a way to cope with the rules.

Because of her illness, Beryl had 74 days to make up, more than the rest of her classmates. After her classmates departed she was fearful that she would be tempted to stay out past the curfew so she begged the school officials for night duty. The administrators could not understand her desire for night work but they assigned her to the night shift anyway. The scheme worked; she graduated.

Barbara Oetzel Lenthart had a difficult time with the rules at her school of nursing in Madison, Wisconsin. She said, "The rules seemed pointless. Our country was involved in a world war with daily shattering news, but we were not allowed radios in our rooms."

The housemother announced she would smell students' breaths when they came in at night to determine if they had been drinking. In order to cope with the inspection, Barbara figured out a way to dissuade the housemother from her proposed action. The nurses' residence was located in the midst of an Italian neighborhood where most residents raised vegetables in their victory gardens. On the way home from a movie, Barbara and her roommate pulled onions from one of the gardens, peeled off the surface to remove the dirt and ate them. The housemother never again smelled students' breaths.

Barbara also broke rules inadvertently. Someone had over-watered the plants and water ran onto the floor. Trying to be helpful and prevent a fall, Barbara grabbed paper towels and swabbed the area. An instructor scolded her for not using a mop. She explained she didn't know where the mop was and that the towels were handy. Her instructor told her to stop making excuses and used the incident to document that Barbara had a bad attitude.

Despite the rules and regulations or maybe because of them, cadet nurses managed to have lots of fun and laughs. Cadet nurse Mary Wilcox Foster of the Robert Packer School of Nursing retired early one evening before "lights out" and was soon sound asleep. The next thing she knew, friends bolted in, told her it was Monday morning and to put her sheets in the laundry. She jumped out of bed, stripped the sheets, and threw the linens down the laundry chute. Then her friends started laughing and she realized it was still evening. That night she slept without sheets. Her friends never let her forget the incident.

Rules and regulations were not always a laughing matter. Several former cadet nurses told of being required to have tonsillectomies before entering the school of nursing even though they had healthy tonsils. Sickness could not be tolerated. Petronella Buck Arledge from Hillcrest Memorial Hospital School of Nursing in Waco, Texas, was hospitalized for minor injuries received from a motorcycle accident. After that, a new rule was added: NO MOTORCYCLE RIDING. Petronella confessed, "That broke up a sweet romance because I could no longer go riding with my boyfriend."

"Rules? We tried to keep them," said Florence Blake Ford. "However, I did break the rule of No Drinking of Alcoholic Beverages when I was a pre-cadet at the Methodist Hospital School of Nursing in Philadelphia."

Florence and her classmates had returned from the Christmas holiday on December 31. To celebrate New Year's Eve someone produced a bottle of wine. The girls went up to the roof to sample it and to listen to the sounds of the city at midnight. They were not caught. Two years later, however, a group of seniors shared a bottle of wine and were not so lucky. The two cadets who instigated the activity completed their training but were not allowed to participate in the graduation exercises.

Young women entering church-affiliated schools of nursing encountered additional religious expectations. Margaret Smith Fairbanks who graduated from the Buffalo Hospital Sisters of Charity School of Nursing, remembered:

> Each morning we attended Mass before going on duty at 7:00 a.m. After Mass we lined up outside the chapel for inspection: spotless uniform; white slip; clean, white shoes; hair off the collar in a hairnet; scissors, pen and procedure book in our uniform pocket; no make-up, jewelry, perfume, or colored nail polish.
>
> We Protestant students were not required to attend Mass but I enjoyed doing so. The sisters and Jesuit priests were saints to tolerate giggling teenage girls. Their stability and professionalism fine-tuned us to become nurse role models ourselves.

Stranger than rules were the protocols regarding relationships, never written, but profoundly understood. "Doctors came first in everything," Florence Blake Ford said. A peculiar ritual occurred countless times a day when hospital personnel observed the order of entering and leaving the elevators. First came the doctors, then the interns, registered nurses, and lastly the students in descending order, from seniors to probies. Ford said, "Pity the other personnel and visitors who became trapped in this obligatory obedience to status and authority."

Junior cadet nurse Lucille North Vogt remembered an unsolved mystery regarding a physician. Dr. Howard Payne, an attending surgeon, lectured to the surgical nursing class at Los Angeles County General Hospital School of Nursing. One morning he arrived, not in the familiar surgical garb, but nattily attired in a suit and tie, looking handsome indeed. A long, low wolf whistle came from somewhere and the entire class was in trouble. The guilty party was asked to step forth and admit her indiscretion. Lucille said, "No one came forward ... so the entire class was campused for a month."

A former cadet nurse recalled a physician who always got off the elevator whistling "Easter Parade." The charge nurse jumped to her feet and stood at rigid attention as if she were hearing the national anthem. Another graduate nurse, one who had worked with General Pershing during World War I, would not allow student nurses to speak directly to physicians. She required the students to speak to her first. She then decided if their concerns or questions merited the attention of the physician. If she deemed the communication worthy, she relayed the message to the physician.

Claribel Carlson Crews remembered an orthopedic surgeon who was difficult to work with, even though he had first trained as a nurse. A group of students at the ward desk heard the surgeon suddenly yell, "Nurse, Nurse!" They raced down the long hall to his aid and he bellowed, "Scissors!"

Simultaneously, they retrieved their scissors from pockets under their aprons. He turned away and said, "Fine. Every good nurse carries her scissors."

"We were so in awe of him," Claribel said. Later, the surgeon was a patient in the hospital, and she cared for him. "He was one of the dearest patients I ever had."

Most of the physicians were understanding and occasionally tried to help the cadet nurses. When the young physicians came back from the war they assumed a collegial relationship with the cadets, shared their war experiences, and brought in fresh techniques. "The hospital would never be the same. Their youthful vigor produced a whole new atmosphere," Claribel said.

Change was beginning in some schools of nursing during the '40s and in those schools nurse and physician relationships were different. "Nurse [and physician] relationships were good at the University of Minnesota School of Nursing," Betty Deming Pearson said. Their head nurses reminded cadets that they were women and should have doors opened for them. They entered the elevators first if the others were not patients, and did not give up their chairs to physicians. When a physician, resident, or intern threw things or became verbally abusive, cadets were instructed to lay the instruments down, even if they were in the operating room, and leave. "Our instructors told us that no doctor deserved a nurse under such circumstances," Betty said.

Betty rotated to the obstetrics ward in another hospital where the obstetrician picked up a rubber suction bulb and found it soft from too many steam sterilizations. He raised his hand, ready to throw the suction bulb at Betty but stopped and asked which hospital she was from. When she answered "the University of Minnesota," the obstetrician put down the bulb. "My school taught me to set standards for behavior when the need arose," Betty recounted.

Dormitory rules and regulations also differed in many schools of nursing associated with colleges and universities compared to more stringent rules at nonuniversity schools. Established in 1909 as the first university school of nursing in the world, the University of Minnesota set a precedent. Cadet Ursula Hanson Hawkins expressed appreciation for her dean, Katharine Densford. This nurse leader petitioned for and received the same rules for cadet nurses as provided for the rest of the university students. After completing the 6-month probationary period, cadets could stay out until midnight any night of the week and could have two 2:00 a.m. time limits as well. A student committee handled infractions.

Densford's argument was this: If a student nurse (who had to be at least 17 years old) was mature enough to be given the responsibility for the vital care of critically ill people, then she should not be restricted like a child in her social life. Densford led the cause for reasonable nurse dormitory rules.

Cadet nurses from the University of Minnesota dared to commit the playful pranks of youth. Albina Borho Reichmuth remembered Mrs. Chase, the life-sized mannequin who was probed, propped, lathered, and washed hundreds of times by cadets in the nursing arts lab. Mrs. Chase once became a target of mischief and was found fully clothed in traditional student-nurse garb, seated on a toilet in the interns' dormitory. Another time, the *Minneapolis Tribune* reported a student nurse had been found hanging in the tower near the armory next door to the nurses' dorm. It was the all-suffering Mrs. Chase.

Cadet nurse Gladys Lund Hughes respected Dean Densford who expected her cadets to take personal responsibility rather than be over-regulated in every aspect of their lives. "After all," Gladys said, "we were accountable for our patients' lives. Why shouldn't we be answerable for our own?" Katharine Densford, striving for her own identity as a woman faculty member with all male colleagues, became a visionary for what nursing education should be in the future.

References

Kalisch, B.J., & Kalisch, P.A. (1975). Slaves, servants, or saints? An analysis of the system of nurse training in the United States, 1873-1948. **Nursing Forum, 14**(3), 246-250.

14

Serving Despite Adversity
by Thelma M. Robinson

I knocked at the door of a little house at the end of the road overlooking Kachemak Bay near Homer, Alaska. Mitsu Hasegawa Nakada greeted me. She steadied her gait with a cane as she led me to the living room. "We bought this home for the view," she said.

A large picture window framed a post card scene. Blue water sparkled in the sun. Across Kachemak Bay stood the majestic Kenai Mountains topped with glaciers that flowed down to the forest below. Friends of the Nakadas were leaving. "You should interview Henry," they said when they learned the purpose of the visit.

Mr. Nakada served as a scout with the 442nd all-Japanese American Regimental Combat Team during World War II. The courageous account of the Army's most decorated military unit has been told again and again. But hundreds of Japanese American women also served in World War II, and I wanted to hear Mitsu's story.

"Sit close," Mitsu said. "We are remodeling and my voice is soft due to Parkinson's." We talked as carpenters pounded and sawed in an adjoining room. Mitsu spoke in low tones telling about times and events as if they happened yesterday.

After the bombing of Pearl Harbor, panic swept the West Coast and Japanese Americans became the focus of anxiety. While no subversive activity was found among those with Japanese ancestry, the public demanded evacuation of

Japanese Americans to the interior regions of the country. President Roosevelt signed Executive Order 9066 on February 19, 1942, which resulted in the transporting of 110,000 Japanese Americans to 10 internment camps scattered among seven states. Sixty per cent of these people were American citizens and 40,000 were children (Myer, 1971).

Japanese American young men found freedom from confinement in an internment camp by volunteering for the armed forces. Their sisters wanted to serve too-some as nurses. The American Friends Service Committee organized the National Japanese American Student Relocation Council, but war hysteria complicated their efforts (Myer, 1971).

In March 1942 Margaret Tracy, director of the University of California School of Nursing in San Francisco, wrote Claribel Wheeler of the National League of Nursing Education for advice. Margaret had 22 students of Japanese descent who were born in America. Scholastically these students were at the top of their classes and the nursing faculty found their performances on the wards above average. Tracy wondered if any schools of nursing in the country might accept these students as transfers.

Claribel had just met with nurse leaders from several professional organizations. They had discussed the problem of Japanese American student nurses and arrived at a consensus. She reported that under the circumstances, the committee doubted if any schools in the United States would be willing to take the Japanese American nurse students (Kalisch & Kalisch, 1974).

In Nebraska during a conference, several nursing school directors asked a consultant from the National Nursing Council for War Service about admitting Japanese American students. The consultant advised against it and said that there would always be mistrust in the minds of patients as well as doctors and nurses (Fagan, 1992).

But the *American Journal of Nursing* reported positive reactions from patients, physicians, and fellow nurse students at the few schools of nursing that had accepted Japanese American women. The journal quoted President Roosevelt who said, "Americanism is not and never was a matter of race or ancestry. Every loyal American citizen should be given the opportunity to serve their country wherever his (or her) skill will make the greatest contribution ("The Problem," 1943, pp. 895-896).

Schools of nursing were urged to find a solution for loyal American girls whose ancestors happened to be Japanese. The U.S. Cadet Nurse Corps encouraged the recruitment of minority students. Opportunities, however, did not come easily for these young women who wanted to serve their country as nurses.

Stories Told by Japanese American Cadets

When the war started, Mitsu Hasegawa was in her first year at the Los Angeles County General Hospital School of Nursing when she read an announcement telling those with Japanese ancestry to meet in the hospital's auditorium. Nearly 500 people, including secretaries, laboratory technicians, physicians, pathologists, x-ray technicians, nurses, and students gathered to learn they would have to leave their schools, jobs, businesses, and homes.

The Japanese Americans had 2 weeks to prepare for their departure and were given permission to take 100 pounds of personal belongings. "We didn't know where we were going," Mitsu said, "and it was hard to plan. I tried to make culottes in case we went to the desert, but I sewed both legs together and couldn't get into them."

The Los Angeles group met at the Hollywood Presbyterian Church on May 10, 1942. Mitsu's roommate and friend came to say good-bye. Tears streamed down her face as she peered through the fence. She said, "But you are like us and we are like you."

Mitsu Hasegawa, with the first group of Japanese American evacuees from the Pomona Army Assembly Center, arrived at the Heart Mountain Relocation Center near Cody, Wyoming, on August 12, 1942. Men with machine guns stood in the towers at each corner of the camp and at the gate. Each evacuee was issued a cot, a mattress, and two blankets. A family's space included a stove and one light bulb but no partition. When a family could spare them, they hung their blankets for privacy. Living became difficult for these quiet, gentle people. "We weren't abused," said Mitzu. "We had plenty of food and we all worked. The hardest part was not knowing how long we would be there."

Because of her 9 months of experience as a student nurse, Mitsu was placed in charge of the hospital's surgical unit at Heart Mountain Relocation Camp. As she was leaving for the camp she remembered seeing a lady with paralysis on a litter being loaded through the window of the train. This woman, Mrs. Nakada, became her patient. Her son Henry, a soldier in the army, was granted a leave to give blood for his mother who was scheduled for surgery. When he returned to his base he sent the nurses a box of chocolates saying, in a note, that he was impressed with the good nursing care his mother had received. This was a special treat for the interned women during sugar rationing. Mitsu responded with a note of thanks, which was the beginning of a romance that continues to this day.

Mitsu worked 1 year at the Heart Mountain Relocation camp proving her loyalty while earning $16 per month. One day she learned about the Corps. With family resources tied up, this was a way for her to finish her training and to do something for her country. She went before the board with her plea and a plan. The Federal Bureau of Investigation cleared her records and the board said yes; she was free to leave.

Mitsu found a job in Chicago as a nurse aide in a home for children with disabilities. She also began a search for a school of nursing that would accept her. Persistence, patience, and time paid off. The Protestant Episcopal Hospital School of Nursing in Philadelphia accepted her as a student and gave her full credit for the 6 months of her previous student nurse course work.

Other Japanese Americans told similar stories about how they became cadet nurses. One of those women was Sharon Tanagi Aburano. While at Minidoka Relocation camp in Hunt, Idaho, Sharon also learned about the Corps. Before the war her family had lived in an integrated community in Seattle, where her father ran a successful grocery store and the family had become members of the Presbyterian Church.

When the Japanese bombed Pearl Harbor, Sharon, a high school student, remembered the FBI coming for her father and other Japanese American community leaders and business people. Although no charges were filed against them, 2 years passed before Mr. Tanagi was reunited with his family. Sharon's brother served at the Military Intelligence School in Minnesota while she and her mother were sent to Idaho. Sharon finished high school at the camp and then worked as a nurse aide.

Father Tibesar, a Catholic Priest from Seattle, followed his "flock" to the Idaho relocation camp and told Sharon about the U.S. Cadet Nurse Corps. He suggested that she apply to the St. Mary's Hospital School of Nursing associated with the famed Mayo Clinic Foundation in Rochester, Minnesota. The priest then wrote a letter to the Franciscan Sisters who operated the school attesting to Sharon's character.

Sharon received a brochure (a possession she cherishes today) with information about the Corps. Here was a chance to prove her patriotism and to acquire a profession. With bank accounts frozen and no income, the Corps provided her an education and paid her as well. She said, "Even though I had to leave my mother behind barbed wire and wondered if I would ever see her again, I could now care for myself and my parents."

Rhoda Behrndt Kite, a cadet nurse from Bellevue Hospital School of Nursing, remembered her Japanese American classmate, Dorothy Kikuye Hayashi. She had been a second year nursing student at the University of California when the war started. Dorothy spent a year interned with her family in California, then at Heart Mountain in Wyoming, before she received permission to relocate. She wanted to finish her nurse's training and went to Chicago to earn money.

Only low paying jobs were available for a nisei (American-born Japanese). Dorothy worked as a maid doing housework for a Chicago family, saving every penny she could from her wages. She learned about the Corps and enrolled in the Bellevue Hospital School of Nursing in New York City. She graduated in June 1946 with a degree as well as a diploma in nursing. Director Tracy of the University of California School of Nursing learned that Dorothy, her former student, had received the Bellevue Alumnae Award for the highest scholarship average and excellence in nursing practice.

Stories Told by Black American Cadets

In late summer of 1943, Florence Jarvis Henderson, a 17-year-old black woman, listened to her radio, which was a high school graduation present from her parents. She heard a startling announcement.

> Girls who are high school graduates, here is the chance of your lifetime. Get free training in the world's proudest profession by joining the U.S. Cadet Nurse Corps. For information go to your local hospital or write to Box 88, New York, NY (USPHS, Division of Nurse Education, Federal Security Agency, 1943).

Working as a nurse aide in Dallas, Texas, Florence had dreamed of becoming a nurse since she was in grade school. But her mother and father, both employed as cooks, had no money to help her attend a school of nursing. Hearing the radio announcement, Florence began her inquiry. In September she walked through the doors of the Tuskegee Institute in Alabama enrolled as a nursing student.

The National Association of Colored Graduate Nurses advised and assisted the Public Health Service in recruiting black women. Three thousand black women enrolled in all-black schools of nursing between 1943 and 1948—a dramatic increase (Kalisch & Kalisch, 1974). Wartime shortages of adequately prepared instructors, housing, and clinical facilities prevented the enrollment from being even higher ("Negro Students," 1944).

In 1944, 25% of all black schools of nursing had a collegiate degree program, while only 10% of white schools had degree programs ("Negro Students," 1944; National Nursing Council, 1944). Black schools were often ahead in other ways as well. The all-black Homer G. Phillips Hospital School of Nursing in St. Louis placed emphasis on a well-rounded personality for their student nurses. Extracurricular activities for black students were a choice of sewing, drama, sports, journalism, book discussions, dancing, and singing ("Negro School," 1940).

Many poorly financed black schools could not meet the Corps standards. Nurse Education Consultant Ruth Johnson of the U.S. Public Health Service said, "It was tough. Some schools didn't have money to provide properly for the new students." She observed cadets using fruit boxes and orange crates to improvise bedside tables and storage for clothing and other possessions. She said, "The cadets worked hard, often under poor circumstances. Those kids in the Cadet Nurse Corps earned every nickel they got" (R. Johnson, personal communication, May 13, 1995).

In order to benefit from the Bolton Act windfall, some all-white schools abandoned their policies of discrimination and admitted black women. In 1941, 29 schools of nursing admitted both black and white students; by the end of World War II the number had increased to 49. The Veterans Facility in Tuskegee, Alabama, was the only government facility to accept black senior cadets (Kalisch & Kalisch, 1974).

However, social and learning opportunities were not always equal for black student nurses. Alma Gault, dean of the school of nursing at the all-black Meharry Medical College in Nashville, Tennessee, contacted the Department of Interior, Indian Affairs reservation hospital requesting assignments for her senior cadet nurses. Despite the students' high standards of work, officials in the Indian Health Service (IHS) turned down the cadets, emphasizing the lack of recreational and social experiences for black women at the reservation hospital. Noting that other black nurse graduates had found adjustment difficult, IHS officials asked if it would be fair to the (black) cadets because the patients themselves, because of misunderstanding or reflecting on the prejudices of others, might show an unwillingness to accept their services (Kalisch & Kalisch, 1974).

Lucille North Vogt, who attended a mixed school of nursing, noted that the black students had their own cottage with a black housemother that was set aside from white students. She loved to visit her black classmates because they were allowed in their kitchen for cookies or other snacks any time they wished.

Lucille thought it was the black students' choice to be together in their own cottage. She wondered why the black cadets didn't participate in some of the white social events but again thought it was their own choice. "It never occurred to me that my friends were not allowed to do everything we were doing."

Periodically, consultant Ruth Johnson visited schools of nursing that accepted both black and white students. The black cadets lived in separate dormitories and usually had special places to eat in the dining rooms. Johnson called this to the hospitals' and nursing administrators' attention and said, "We don't do this anymore." Johnson added, "I don't know if it did any good, but I felt I had to say something. You don't demean anyone like that. I didn't like it!"

Names were important to the black cadets attending St. Philip Hospital School of Nursing in Richmond, Virginia. The cadets always called each other "Miss" followed by their last name to discourage physicians calling them by

Despite her excellent school grades, Sarah Gomez Erlach encountered discrimination against Hispanics. After graduation from high school, she could not get a job. The San Bernadino County Hospital School of Nursing (California) had no ethnic barriers and made it possible for Erlach to achieve her goal of becoming a nurse. She served 34 years in the U.S. Army Nurse Corps, retired a full colonel, and is well known for her contributions to migrant health.

their first names. Jessie Jackson Thompson said, "All the doctors were white and there was no social interaction, but professionally we communicated well."

What happened to the black 17-year-old woman who was promised a lifetime education? Well, Florence Jarvis Henderson taught nursing for 50 years. She encouraged men and women to enter the nursing profession, to complete their education, and to pass their final test for licensure. When talking to young people, Florence said she always emphasized the importance of exchanging a paycheck for a welfare check.

Stories Told by Hispanic American Cadets

Sarah Gomez Erlach was at the "end of her rope" when she graduated from high school because she could not get a job. She lived in Southern California and experienced what Hispanics across the nation were going through, discrimination.

Sarah wanted to be a nurse, a desire she had had from an early age because of the influence of her mother. She saw how her mother cared for family members when they were ill including two cousins with TB. Her mother cared for these teenagers in their home using "isolation," rest, and nutrition. They recovered and lived to be over 80 years of age.

Sarah finally got a job with the government-sponsored National Youth Corps counting cars coming into San Bernardino. But Sarah wanted more than this; she wanted a career. She read in a local newspaper about a scholarship to a local school of nursing. She went to the dean of the school of nursing with her record of having an "A" average and her story of discrimination.

The scholarship was for $100 but had to be matched by that same amount. Family members all pitched in and raised $55. Years later Sarah found out her mother raised the remaining $45 by collecting on past-due loans that friends and neighbors owed her father. "Collecting" was taboo in the Mexican culture, but her mother resolutely asked each to pay what they could and thus came up with the needed amount. The scholarship helped Sarah begin her nurse education. The Corps option also became available and further helped her solve her financial problem.

Stories Told by Native American Cadets

A Sister from the Presentation School of Nursing wondered why Bertha Marshall Gipp, a Lakota Sioux Indian, began to cry when told that she was accepted as a student. Bertha lived on an Indian reservation in South Dakota and had dreamed of being a nurse since she was 8 years old.

Alyce Valandry, a Sioux Indian, and Rowena Tentewa, a Hopi, officiate at the launching of the S.S. Coastal Nomad at the Consolidated Steel Company Shipyards in Wilmington, California, on July 9, 1945. Both cadets are from Sage Memorial School of Nursing in Ganado, Arizona.

Now the Corps made it possible for her to fulfill her dream and tears of joy streamed down her face.

Bertha remembered the 150-mile train ride from Kenel to Aberdeen, South Dakota, sitting on her suitcase on a crowded train filled with servicemen. Excited but also frightened, she wondered what lay ahead. As the train pulled into the station, Bertha saw six Caucasian girls, all her age and smiling as they held up a big sign that read,

"WELCOME BERTHA MARSHALL." One of the girls approached her and said, "Bertha, is that you?"

For the next 3 years, these young women studied, worked, cried, and laughed together, learning what it meant to be a nurse, and building a bond that would last a lifetime. After graduation Bertha continued to serve her people in the Dakotas as a nurse. In 1994 she received the honor of American Indian Woman of Excellence in Health, just one of many awards she received throughout her career of 50 years.

The Board of National Missions of the Presbyterian Church recognized the difficulties for Native American young women who grew up on a reservation and wanted to serve their people as nurses. In 1930 the church established the Sage Memorial Hospital School of Nursing in Ganada, Arizona. Located in the heart of the Navajo Reservation, the modern, well-equipped hospital provided medical care for all tribes as well as for all other people who lived in the isolated area. The Native Americans appreciated the skilled Native American trained nurses who gave a much-needed service to their people (Kalisch & Kalisch, 1995).

In 1945, 40 young women were enrolled in the Sage Hospital School of Nursing, representing 25 tribes from 12 states. Almost all of these young women joined the U.S. Cadet Nurse Corps. They found the stipends given made them relatively rich in an area that was desperately poor (Kalisch & Kalisch, 1995).

A special honor was in store for two Native American cadet nurses, both students at the Sage School of Nursing.

On July 9, 1945, cadet nurses Alyce Valandry, a Sioux, and her maid-of-honor, Rowena Pentewa, a Hopi, launched the S.S. Coastal Nomad in Wilmington, California. When the ship slid down into the water, Chief Richard Davis Thunderbird gave a war hoop ("Nomad and Namesake," 1945).

Stories Told by Male Nurses

Among minority nurses who suffered the greatest indignities during World War II were the men who chose nursing as their profession. In the early 1940s only four accredited schools of nursing admitted male students. During this time, only 63 of 1,300 schools of nursing admitted both men and women students. Men have given nursing care dating back to the Crusades and to the Dark Ages during the black plague. But men in nursing suffered humiliation during World War II.

When the war came, Jacob Rose, RN, a recent graduate from Bellevue Hospital School of Nursing, requested that his 3 years of nurse training be applied to service in the military. He pointed out the country's desperate need for nurses, the threat of a draft of women nurses, and the huge sums of money spent urging women to volunteer as nurse aides. Jacob ended up driving a dump truck for the Army filling potholes in Ledo, India (Rose, 1947).

Male nurses often hid their nurse training background and accomplished more through other duties with the military. Those who acknowledged their nursing experience often served as privates while their female counterparts served as officers.

During World War II, federal monies were available for training men to be physicians and pilots. What about men who wanted to take advantage of belonging to the U.S. Cadet Nurse Corps? At least one man succeeded. He sent this letter dated July 6, 1944, to the editor of the *New York Times*:

A news item in your issue of July 1 pertaining to the Cadet Nurse Corps states that the recruits are all young women. The Cadet Nurse Corps is open to young men as well, proof of which I am a member of the Corps, being entered Feb. 1, 1944. Emanuel Goldberg, Queens Village, L.I. ["Male Cadet," 1944].

President Roosevelt's plea that every person should serve his country, wherever his (or her) skill would make the greatest contribution, often was not available to people of minority groups. The Corps enhanced opportunities in nursing for a few Japanese, Black, Hispanic, and Native American young women. But during World War II, men who chose nursing as their profession often found it a dead-end as a way of serving their country. Noble statements are easily made but the test comes in making good things happen.

References

Fagan, M.L. (1992, Fall). Nebraska nursing education during World War II. **Nebraska History**, p. 132.
Kalisch, P.A., & Kalisch, B.J. (1995). **The advance of American nursing**, (3rd ed., pp. 400-401). Boston: Little Brown.
Kalisch, P.A., & Kalisch, B.J. (1974). **The study of the impact of U.S. cadet nurse corps on the American nursing professional through an historical analysis and synthesis.** (Vol. 1 of Final Report of NIH Grant NU 00443, pp. 110-114, 627, 647-649).
Male cadet nurse also. (1944, July 6). **New York Times**, p. 14.
Myer, D.S. (1971). **Uprooted Americans: The Japanese Americans and the war relocation authority during World War II** (p. xxvi). Tucson, AZ: The University of Arizona Press.
National Nursing Council for War Service. (1944, September). Colleges and universities offering an undergraduate program leading to both a diploma in nursing and a degree, and schools of nursing connected with colleges and universities (RG90). Washington, DC: National Archives and Records Administration.
Negro students in the U.S. cadet nurse corps. (1944). **American Journal of Nursing, 44**(9), 887.
Negro school has fine system of orientation. (1940, June). **Cadet Nurse Corps News,**1, p. 3. (Cadet Nurse File). Bethesda, MD: National Library of Medicine.
Nomad and namesake. (1945, September). **Cadet Nurse Corps News,** 1 p. 4. (Cadet Nurse File). Bethesda, MD. National Library of Medicine.
Rose, J. (1947). Men nurses in military service. **American Journal of Nursing, 47**(1), 146.
The problem of student nurses of Japanese ancestry. (1943). **American Journal of Nursing, 43**(11), 895-896.
USPHS, Division of Nurse Education, Federal Security Agency. (1943). **What school will you choose? U.S. cadet nurse corps.** (Cadet Nurse File). Bethesda, MD: National Library of Medicine.

15

The War Is Over!
by Paulie M. Perry

> The war is over, thank God! Everyone is busy celebrating, horns honking, people cheering, but I feel more like just thinking. I'm so thankful it's over at last.

This diary entry for Tuesday, August 14, 1945, described my feelings. Our family attended a church service dedicated to peace and prayed for the safe return of my brother, Wally, from his secret naval assignment in China.

I had received my acceptance to Lincoln General Hospital School of Nursing just 4 days before V-J (Victory over Japan) Day. My excitement in preparing to leave home was clouded with the concern about whether the U.S. Cadet Nurse Corps would continue in peacetime.

Cadets experienced the emotions of V-J Day in a variety of ways. My sister, Thelma, a junior cadet at Lincoln General Hospital School of Nursing, and a soldier friend were watching a movie matinee when they heard a commotion. The theater manager stopped the movie and announced that World War II had ended. Thelma's date left the theater to check out the activities in the streets. He returned in half an hour excitedly telling of servicemen buying and changing into civilian clothes. "He excused himself from our date to join the frivolity. I road the bus back to the dorm by myself," Thelma said.

Junior cadet Alice Jans Donley vividly remembered that day as one of joy and celebration:

When I heard the news in lab class I stood up, cheered, and clapped. After class the cadet nurses of the Sioux Valley Hospital School of Nursing ran out of the building and rang the bells in the campanile, then rode the bus downtown to revel in the joy that the war was over. Airmen from the nearby Army air base crowded onto Main Street, dancing and singing. We joined in the fun.

Later we put on our cadet nurse uniforms and walked in the parade. We walked because we had no training in marching. We just showed up in uniform and followed orders.

Senior cadet Marilyn Busk Hutcherson of the University of Minnesota said, "Our chief nurse at Camp Carson, Colorado, served in the Philippines and suffered that fateful Bataan experience. She gave all the nurses 3 days off after V-J Day. What a time of celebration we had. We borrowed a car and drove up to the 14,110-foot summit of Pike's Peak and then went to the officers' club, excited over the news."

Junior cadet Mary Rupel, who had night duty at Lubbock General Hospital in Texas, had a very different experience. She recalled:

Those of us on night duty slept until 2:00 p.m. and were unaware of the peace agreement. We walked a mile to the park for 2 hours of relaxation. On our hike back to the dorm we were amazed at the number of cars bumper to bumper. Drivers honked their horns and passengers waved, yelled, and laughed. We didn't know what prompted all the commotion, but when we found out the reason for their elation we too became jubilant.

After junior cadet Betty Cheney Sexton got off duty at the Colorado General Hospital at 9:00 p.m., she took the trolley to 16th and Champa in downtown Denver to see what was going on. People jammed the streets and general chaos abounded as hundreds of citizens celebrated. Strangers hugged each other, kissed, and danced. "I found it frightening," she said.

Then, like a miracle, a voice out of her past said, "What in the world are you doing here?" Betty turned and saw a soldier. She immediately recognized her friend, Tom, from high school.

They had graduated together. He entered the service in 1942 and she joined the Corps the following year. She and Tom had a wonderful visit, elated and shocked at the surprise meeting. Tom made certain that Betty got on the streetcar heading back to Colorado General Hospital. "I let the people in the streets continue their revelry while I celebrated getting back to my dorm safe and sound."

Not everyone could join the revelers. Patients in hospitals continued to need care. On V-J Day junior cadet Barbara Oetzel Lenthart worked the 3:00 - 11:00 p.m. shift at Madison General Hospital and knew nothing about the victory when she went on duty. As Barbara charted nurse notes near the window that was kept open to get a breeze during the hot season, she noticed a man in uniform on the street below. He was running, leaping, and shouting for joy. No one on the unit knew the reason for his behavior. Later she found a patient with a radio who had heard the news. "Then I, too, became as excited as the patient with the radio and the man in the uniform in the streets," Barbara said.

Junior cadet Dorothie Melvin Crowley remembered V-J also.

On that day I worked alone as charge nurse on a men's surgical convalescent ward at Los Angeles County General Hospital on the 3:00 - 11: 00 p.m. shift. One of my 20 patients, who listened to the earphone radio, told me the news of the war's end. I couldn't believe it.

So I went to an empty patient room and grabbed one of the radio earphones off the wall and listened to an excited reporter tell the reactions to peace from all over the world. Dropping the earphone I ran from room to room telling the patients. Usually a shy, reserved girl, I forgot myself in sharing the happy news. My non-ambulatory patients and I couldn't physically dance in the halls, but our hearts danced.

Not all Americans reacted to V-J Day with frivolity. Betty Allen Kinner, a junior cadet, heard the news of the war's end while on duty at St. Mary's Hospital in Huntington, West Virginia. "The news reporters told of a new type of bomb that had been used," Betty recalled. Although jubilant over the war's end, the cadets wondered what this bomb meant to the world if it could create such destruction. "We gathered for a discussion of these concerns after we got off work," Betty said.

Some cadet nurses heard about the war's end while traveling. Phyllis Musich, a pre-cadet at Henry Ford Hospital School of Nursing in Detroit, Michigan, and a friend were traveling to her home in upper Michigan when they heard about the war's end.

> We heard the radio announcement of the peace agreement in our downtown hotel. My friend had a brother in the Far East and I had brothers who were still in Europe. So we were very excited about the news. We opened the window to view the excitement below while we shed copious tears of relief.

Still grieving for her brother who was killed in action in Germany, senior cadet Anne Higgins Murphy worked a regular shift at Flower-Fifth Avenue Hospital in New York City on V-J Day. "Most of the staff wanted to go to Times Square," Anne said. "Although I was glad the war was over, I could not bear to participate in the celebration. Instead I worked extra duty so friends could be part of the excitement."

The end of the war raised questions for the young women who planned to enter the Corps as pre-cadets in September 1945. Cadets currently enrolled in the Corps were also concerned and asked, "Will we be allowed to finish our nurse training?" Junior cadets wondered if they could serve in a military hospital during their last 6 months and senior cadets now felt uncertain about their plans to enlist in one of the branches of service at graduation (U.S. Federal Security Agency, Public Health Service, 1950).

Recruitment to the Corps ended at once, but plans were needed for the orderly cessation of the vast program. Corps Director Lucile Petry (Leone) said:

Japanese surrender does not automatically end new admissions of cadet nurses. All cadet nurses are urged to stand by and await official announcement of the date of the cessation of hostilities, which will determine the date after which those entering the Corps would not receive full scholarships ("V-J Day," 1945, p. 682).

Section 10 of Public Law 74, 78th Congress stated, "The Nurse Training Program (Cadet Nurse Corps) shall cease to be in effect upon the date of the termination of hostilities in the present war as determined by the President" (U.S. Federal Security Agency, 1950, p. 77). National leaders immediately planned for an orderly transition.

Senator Elbert D. Thomas, democrat from Utah and Surgeon General Parran sent recommendations to President Truman for continuing the U.S. Cadet Nurse Corps. They urged that

PROGRAM SUPPORT CENTER, DEPARTMENT OF HEALTH AND HUMAN SERVICES

In July 1945 in Independence, Missouri, President Truman and Cadet Helen Hinde reviewed plans for the U.S. Cadet Nurse Corps. When the war ended in August 1945, Mr. Truman authorized a gradual phase out of the Corps from 1945 to 1948.

the 100,000 cadet nurses currently in training be allowed to complete their courses and that the 30,000 young women scheduled to begin training in the early fall of 1945 be permitted to take the full course ("Ask End of Cadet Nursing," 1945).

After considerable discussion with Congress and Surgeon General Parran, President Truman announced all new enrollments in the Cadet Nurse Corps would end October 15, 1945. The fall class was saved! President Truman said:

> The United States Cadet Nurse Corps has contributed greatly to meeting the needs of the nation for nurses, military and civilian. The Corps has made a substantial contribution to health in wartime. Its graduates will continue in the ways of peace to serve the health needs of our veterans and the civilian population ("Federal Aid Continues," 1945, p. 1).

President Truman declared the cessation of hostilities on December 31, 1946, bringing the Cadet Nurse Corps to an official end.

My classmates and I, who entered Lincoln General Hospital School of Nursing in September 1945, gave a "hip hooray" with the news that we would be cadets after all and receive the full benefits of the Corps except for the uniform. However, we could borrow a cadet uniform from a big sister or friend to get a discount at a movie or to have a special picture taken. Postwar cadets wore the Maltese cross patch on the left sleeve of the student uniform, designating them as official members of the Corps.

As soon as the fabric became available for civilian use after wartime shortages, styles of women's clothing changed. A more feminine fashion, with the full, flowing, mid-calf skirts of the Gibson-girl style appeared. Nevertheless, the next year, Lincoln General Hospital junior nurse cadets were dismayed and angry when school of nursing officials sold the leftover inventory of cadet suits, coats, and purses to the new probies-who weren't even cadet nurses-and to non-nurse hospital employees. We were irate that we junior cadets were not given first choice to purchase cadet attire.

Because new cadet nurses were disappointed they would not receive the official outdoor uniform, Mrs. Norman Parsons, the mother of a cadet nurse, wrote the following article, which appeared in the January 1946 issue of the Cadet Nurse Corps News:

To Jean, on her disappointment at not getting her cadet uniform:
So today brought disappointment to my little nurse-to-be?
Our good old Uncle Sammy had to "call a halt," did he?
No doubt he feels his share is done when he provides the books
It's up to ma and pa and you to worry 'bout the "looks."
And that, I'd say, is fair enough, and no calamity
You'll still be mighty sweet to us, and just as fair to see!
And that fine day when you are capped
Our heart will swell with pride,
And joy for you will be greater, too,
Than a uniform could provide.
Of course, it would be swell, I know, to strut in uniform
And after all you'll get that, too, but in another form!
For what could give more joy to be and what a prettier sight
Than a cheerful, happy little nurse in a uniform of white!
So thanks to good old Uncle Sam for helping us at all-
He might have closed his books, you know,
And never heard our call.
So uniform-or-not, go on! Work for the one all-white
And before you know, all 3 years will go,
And you'll be a nurse all right!   Mom
("More About Uniforms," 1946, p. 4).

Dorothy Heiliger Mericle and Dora Handley Cunningham, cadets at the Lincoln General Hospital School of Nursing, posed for a picture wearing borrowed cadet nurse uniforms. "We had only one pair of gloves between us," Dorothy said, "so Dora wore the right one and I wore the left one with our other arms hidden."

Margaret Meyer Nelson entered the Cadet Nurse Corps in 1944 at the University of Minnesota. She said:

As the war ended in 1945, our class did not have any group appearances in our cadet uniforms. My twin sister and I wore our uniforms downtown for pictures, this being the only time we were in complete uniform. After October of 1945 when the Corps no longer recruited students, we stripped down our uniforms and wore the coats over our hospital uniforms.

Corps Director Lucile Petry said:

> With the rapid demobilization of women in the armed services, the national spotlight is no longer focused on uniforms. Rather than assign your cadet nurse uniforms to mothballs-and oblivion-you can make them over into attractive civilian suits.... Remove the epaulets and pocket tabs; change the buttons. If you want more complete variation, remove the collar and lapels-you will have a good looking cardigan suit. Remove the epaulets from your reefer, add a fur collar; consider dyeing all three pieces an exciting new color (Petry, 1946, p. 2).

Cadet nurse Mildred Schepers Genton from Butterworth Hospital School of Nursing in Grand Rapids, Michigan, joined the Army Nurse Corps after her June 1945 graduation. She held overseas orders for the Pacific area on V-J Day with deployment from Camp McCoy, Wisconsin, scheduled in a few days. "What a time of celebration and thanksgiving," Mildred said, "when my overseas orders were cancelled."

Patricia Ruby Morse had great hopes that she could serve her senior cadet period in a military hospital.

> I [had] strongly considered volunteering for the Navy when I finished my training at the University of Minnesota School of Nursing but with the end of the war all of that changed. Senior cadets were no longer needed in military hospitals. Instead I worked as a night charge nurse on a urology unit.

Many nurses coming home from the armed services sought additional education at the university, working part-time while taking classes. "As we neared our December 1947 graduation the hospital had sufficient staff and we wondered if we could find jobs," Patricia said.

Not all military nurses returned to hospital nursing.

Colleges and universities attracted ex-military nurses seeking further education through the GI Bill of Rights. The nationwide shortage of nurses continued in the postwar years, due in part to the high hospital census caused by veterans who needed rehabilitation, many new births, and the increased enrollment in health insurance, which brought hospital care within the financial reach of more Americans (Amidon, 1941). Some nurse veterans married and quit nursing, staying home to raise their families. Other nurses, pressed into active nursing during the war, resumed their inactive status after V-J Day.

In his letter to senior cadets in the Cadet Nurse Corps News, September 1945, Surgeon General Thomas Parran paid tribute to all cadet nurses:

> Dear Senior Cadet:
> At this time I should like to congratulate all members of the Cadet Nurse Corps, especially those of you who are senior cadets ... I have heard nothing but praise for your contributions to America at war ... The Public Health Service is confident that you will justify the faith placed in you when you entered the Corps.... We have not passed the crisis in our needs for civilian nursing service. It is imperative that every one of you as young graduates accepts a position which is essential to our nursing service in this (continued) national emergency.... On the whole health front we still have a tremendous task to do. It is important that all of us do our share. I am looking to you, as is our whole nation, to continue to maintain our essential civilian nursing service at a safe level (Parran, 1945, p. 2).

The cadets in the postwar years did not think about the challenge to maintain a high level of nursing, helping to alleviate the shortage of nurses, or the total national need for nurses to care for patients everywhere ("Many Opportunities," 1946). They were tired from working a busy shift in the hospital, then coming back to the nurses' residence to relax a bit before studying for an upcoming test. They were too tired to be aware of the important part they played in national health care.

References

Amidon, B. (1941). **Better nursing for America** (Pub. Affairs Pamphlet #10).

Ask end of cadet nursing. (1945, August 22). **The New York Times**, p. 12, (RG90).Washington DC: National Archives and Records Administration.

Federal aid continues for Cadet Nurse Corps members. (1945). **Cadet Nurse Corps News**, 1(4), 1. (Cadet Nurse File). Bethesda, MD: National Library of Medicine.

More about uniforms. (1946). [Letter to the Editor.] **Cadet Nurse Corps News**, 1(6), 4.

Many opportunities await cadet nurse corps graduation. (1946). **Cadet Nurse Corps News**, 1(10), 2.

Parran, T. (1945). Required reading. **Cadet Nurse Corps News**, 1(4), 2.

Petry, L. (1946). Memo to you. **Cadet Nurse Corps News**, 1(6), 2.

U.S. Federal Security Agency. (1950). **The U.S. cadet nurse corps 1943-1948**. (PHS Publication No. 38, p. 77). Washington, DC: United States Government Printing Office.

V-J Day and after. (1945). **American Journal of Nursing, 45(12)**, 682.

Wartime nursing is different. (1943). **American Journal of Nursing, 43(9)**, 835-838.

16

Students With Stature: Senior Cadet Nurses
by Paulie M. Perry

"Determined to go west, two classmates and I from the University of Minnesota School of Nursing applied to the Indian Health Service for our senior cadet experience," recalled Shirley Anderson Kastner. "We expected to go to sunny, warm Arizona but where was our assignment? An Indian reservation in North Dakota near the Canadian border where winters were as long and cold as those in Minnesota."

Senior cadet Shirley and her classmates were among the many cadets who extended their nursing boundaries beyond their home hospitals. The U.S. Cadet Nurse Corps provided for these innovative and stimulating experiences by shortening the pre-cadet and junior periods to 30 months. For the last 6 months senior cadets could observe or practice to build their knowledge in areas of patient care not included in the basic curriculum, such as rehabilitation, psychiatry, communicable disease, or rural health care.

The Minnesota cadets arrived at Turtle Mountain Indian Reservation, a desolate, poverty-stricken settlement with the nearest town 20 miles away. The Chippewa or Ojibway Native Americans were one of the largest tribes in North America. The cadets relied on mail order catalogs to do their shopping. They learned to square dance, which became a highlight of their social life.

The cadets observed the stoicism of the Native American women, particularly during childbirth. Shirley made a pledge to herself to have that same kind of fortitude if she ever became pregnant. "I developed a high regard for this hearty group of people," she said.

The meals on the reservation included only one kind of meat—buffalo. "The buffalo meat while nutritious was tough and came from cutting out the old animals in the Yellowstone herd," said Shirley.

Other senior cadet nurses took advantage of the opportunities to expand their nursing expertise not only in the Indian Health Service but also in military hospitals, veterans' hospitals, rural communities, and public health agencies. Senior cadets held positions of responsibility in their home hospitals as well. Years later Assistant Surgeon General Lucile Petry Leone, USPHS (retired), and former director of the Corps, called these periods of discovery and growth "stretching our cadets' horizons."

Another purpose of the senior cadet period was to increase the number of nurses available for service during the wartime shortage of nurses. Senior cadet nurses could be moved to the places where they were most needed thereby providing a more equitable distribution of nursing service throughout the

Cadets arrived with bags and baggage at Tilden General Hospital, Fort Dix, New Jersey, in March 1945. Their faces reflected their enthusiasm for new experiences as senior cadets.

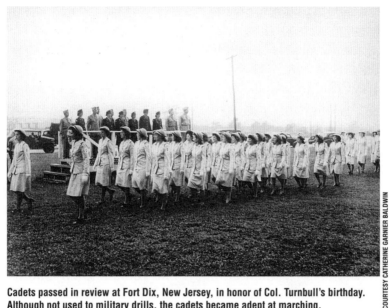

Cadets passed in review at Fort Dix, New Jersey, in honor of Col. Turnbull's birthday. Although not used to military drills, the cadets became adept at marching.

country. Thus the senior period provided advanced learning through the challenge of new experiences and greater responsibility, but was not considered an affiliation (Petry, 1944a).

Senior assignments outside of the home hospital could vary from 3 to 6 months. Releasing students from school facilities made possible the increased recruitment of other cadet nurses. Sound planning made this possible through the cooperation of the school of nursing, the state board of nursing, and the receiving institution (Petry, 1944b).

The USPHS also recruited senior cadet nurses. Their wartime brochure emphasized:

> The dead and wounded are grim consequences of war. As the casualty lists lengthen, as our operating rooms and wards fill with suffering men, the cost of battle grows. Only immediate, skillful nursing can cut this cost and enable these men to return to worthwhile living in a peaceful world.... Yes, you senior cadets are needed in our Marine Hospitals. Can we count on you? (USPHS, Circa 1944).

Senior cadet Martha Crews McBurney of Vanderbilt University School of Nursing in Nashville, Tennessee, is one who answered that call. She said, "While serving in the U.S. Marine Hospital in Staten Island, New York, we also cared for refugees from Eastern Europe. We observed various new diseases and the effect that starvation and hardship produced on people from war areas."

When Corps Director Lucile Petry made a visit to the Marine Hospital she recognized cadet Martha McBurney from her trip to Vanderbilt University the previous year. "What a special treat to be remembered and to talk with her," Martha said.

The town of Council Bluffs, Iowa, held a going-away party at the Strand Theater for June Pyetski Heitman and seven of her classmates from Jennie Edmundson Memorial Hospital School of Nursing. The senior cadets, wearing their winter uniforms, responded to the good wishes of the citizens by singing the Cadet Nurse Corps hymn.

> We wore our uniforms riding the train to Schick Army Hospital in Clinton, Iowa, and frequently during our 3 months at Schick. We had strict daily routines, with stern nurse captains and lieutenants in charge. We learned how to use gas masks and participated in flag ceremonies the same as the GIs did during their basic training.
>
> We loved the hospital at Schick and felt good about caring for our injured war heroes. I also frequently served as circulating nurse in the operating room, helping with the repair of many scars.

June received $60 per month at Schick Army Hospital and considered it a bargain to pay the hospital $30 for her food. "Thanks to the cadet stipend, I purchased my long chiffon wedding dress for $19.95, my veil for $10.95, and a pretty pink lace nightgown for $3.99 in preparation for my wedding 2 weeks after graduation," June said.

Another cadet remembered her great experience at Kennedy General, a large Army hospital in Georgia. She thought the cadet nurses looked especially "military" when they marched in uniform to the ceremonies every Friday where wounded soldiers received their Purple Heart medals. An Army sergeant taught them to march properly at their weekly drills.

While the cadets attended lectures, they often learned more by observing their patients and seeing the courage and spirit of the men with paraplegia. These veterans of the war raced down curved ramps in wheel chairs, fell out, and climbed back in to race again. As therapy, the cadets gave deep muscle massage to the paralyzed legs of the servicemen they cared for. Time and time again patients would reach down to pinch the cadet nurse's leg to see if he could startle her.

Cadets gave, on order, an ounce of whiskey to soldier patients in an effort to stimulate their appetites. The patients pretended to drink the whiskey, but the cadets observed that they stored it in their bedside tables until they had enough to get drunk.

There was not a dry-eyed cadet when it came time to return to the home hospital. The men with paraplegia had strong arms and the cadets couldn't get away without being hugged and kissed.

Senior cadet nurse Camilla Ecklund Johnson said, "I spent my last 6 months at the United States Naval Base Hospital in Seattle, Washington, giving bedside care to many young injured sailors and marines." Although saddened by the war injuries they encountered, the senior cadets enjoyed the pleasant change from the home hospital routine at the University of Minnesota.

The cadets had military inspection on the wards each week, attended military classes, and ate in the women officers' dining hall, which was formally set with white tablecloths and napkins. "We relished the royal treatment, especially savoring the best home-made fresh peach and vanilla ice cream I have ever eaten," Camilla said.

Senior cadet Grace Davis from Stanford University School of Nursing worked with corpsmen and Army nurses when assigned to Letterman Hospital at the Presidio in San Francisco. Grace vividly recalled when a critically ill patient suddenly called out, "Nurse I'm dying, I'm dying!"

Startled, I wondered what I should do. Get oxygen? Call the doctor? The Army lieutenant did neither. Instead she hurried to the patient and held him in her arms. He died.

I learned two things from this military nurse: first, the sacred thing about being a nurse is that we are often with people during their critical life events; second, always listen to the patient.

"I spent the last 6 months as a senior cadet at the Veterans' Psychiatric Hospital in Downey, Illinois, adjacent to the Great Lakes Training facility," Patricia Pasbach said. In the '40s the VA hospitals had difficulty obtaining sufficient staff and depended on corpsmen to balance the staffing of nurses.

A group of corpsmen, returning from the South Pacific war zone and assigned to the VA hospital, resented this tour of duty until they discovered cadet nurses were assigned there, making it not such a bad assignment after all. Many romances and a marriage between a corpsman and a cadet nurse were the result.

Insulin shock therapy was one of the psychiatric treatments at the VA hospital and cadets rotating through this treatment ward reported for duty at 4:00 a.m. to administer the insulin. Not being an early riser, Patricia Pasbach was afraid she would oversleep. "I set three alarm clocks to be sure that I would report to duty on time," she recalled.

Senior cadet Faye Clark Berzon of Beth Israel Hospital School of Nursing spent her last 6 months with the Boston Visiting Nurse Association.

I wore the VNA uniform and had patient assignments just like the other nurses in the office. One day a mother called wanting a nurse to give her little boy a bath as he was recovering from pneumonia. Since the residence was in my district I made the home visit.

When I rang the doorbell and the mother answered she seemed reluctant to let me come in. When the mother finally opened the door I discovered the reason for her hesitation. I had just turned 20 and the "little boy" was a strapping six-footer and 18 years old.

Lorraine Dobmeier Jacobson with 12 other senior cadets from the University of Minnesota went to Virginia, Minnesota, to work at a 60-bed county hospital. They experienced rural nursing and were housed in private homes. After orientation to the hospital and the community, Lorraine was assigned her work areas: the operating room, obstetrics, medical and surgical stations. In obstetrics she worked in the labor and delivery wards with an average of one to two deliveries a day. She said:

I learned how to give ether to mothers for anesthesia by dropping it into the mask over their noses. I worked alone most of the time with only on-call assistance.

I [also] spent 1 day a week in the outpatient department. I went with the public health nurse to visit the Sioux Indians at the Red Lake Reservation. We checked on TB patients, new babies, child immunizations, and heart and diabetic patients and made certain they had adequate food supplies.

Although many of her classmates had gone to Madigan Army Hospital 10 miles from Tacoma, Washington, for their senior cadet experience, Jeanne Riplinger Worthington chose to remain at Tacoma General Hospital. The first 3 months she was a scrub nurse for several physicians who performed major surgery. "One of my classmates and I were the only senior cadets in surgery, and we delighted in working with persnickety doctors in the most complicated assignments," she remembered. She also said:

I spent the last 3 months on night duty working alone in the emergency rooms and setting up for morning surgeries. On V-J Day the whole city went wild and I had to call for help in ER, as accident victims came in all night long.

"For my senior cadet period I requested Public Health in Nashville, Tennessee," Claribel Carlson Crews recalled. The director of nurses at Lincoln General Hospital School of Nursing discouraged her, saying that six additional months at her home school would be of more value. Claribel said:

> I followed her advice and have never been sorry for that decision. I had 6 weeks' experience in communicable disease at Children's Hospital in Denver, worked as a supervisor, and served additional time in every department, including the emergency room. That 6 months proved invaluable throughout my nursing career.

My sister Thelma's goal was to spend her last 6 months as a senior cadet in the New York Henry Street Settlement. Both she and her roommate completed their applications and submitted them on schedule, as directed, to the director of nurses. They waited patiently with another senior cadet who wanted to serve with the Indian Health Services.

The deadline for approval passed and the director told Thelma and her classmates that she had overlooked their applications. The director then assigned Thelma to central supply, where she served as assistant head nurse amid the enema tubing and steam from the autoclave. But at least there was no night duty. "I shared every other Sunday off with the head nurse, plus the love of my life was soon to come home from the war. The reasonable hours made it possible for me to see him often," said Thelma.

Two of Thelma's classmates, Janet Howerter McLaughlin and Shirley Johnson Hanek, wanted a senior cadet experience in public health nursing. They submitted their applications directly to Vanderbilt University School of Nursing in Tennessee and were accepted.

They packed their bags, dressed in their Corps uniforms, and boarded a train to Nashville. Six months later, just a few days before graduation, they arrived back at their home hospital, exuberant and enriched from their senior cadet experience. Thelma said, "My two classmates taught me a lesson in assertiveness."

Schools of nursing were responsible for planning the senior cadet period but many school directors were more concerned with staffing their home hospitals than with offering cadets an alternative learning experience. Urging wider use of senior cadets, Corps Director Lucile Petry wrote to one hospital administrator on July 14, 1944, "We must depend on school directors to realize that other hospitals need senior cadets. By assigning senior cadets elsewhere, schools have more facilities for expanding their own enrollments and they are making a fine contribution to the war effort (U.S. Federal Security Agency, 1950).

More than one disgruntled administrator complained. Senior nurses had become extremely valuable assets to the economy of hospitals. Now the USPHS asked them to offer senior cadets a choice, which could include an experience away from the home hospital school of nursing. Statistics showed that 73% of all senior cadets spent their last 6 months in their home hospitals (U.S. Federal Security Agency, 1950).

Coming along 2 years after Thelma and with the war now over, my classmates and I from Lincoln General Hospital had different experiences for our senior year than did Thelma and her classmates. I spent 2 weeks working at White Hall, a state orphanage, 6 weeks in public health, and 6 weeks in the communicable disease department of the Children's Hospital in Denver, Colorado.

In Denver, I cared for patients with meningitis, encephalitis, pertussis (whooping cough), and complications from measles and mumps. When I heard a baby going into a choking and whooping spell, I hurriedly put on my isolation gown and started the suction machine to remove the sticky mucous from the baby's throat. One adorable baby was a happy tyke, but every time she laughed, it triggered a paroxysmal cough. I remember that each time she had a coughing spell she nearly died and if she had, a part of me would have died with her. It broke my heart to see her so ill.

In following isolation technique, we wore masks, caps, and gowns-and we washed our hands repeatedly. My hands turned painfully red and raw and frequently bled from the irritation of scrubbing with harsh soap and water.

One of my classmates contracted mumps from a patient and remained at Children's an additional month to make up the time she lost while hospitalized. "I had nothing to do but study and as a result, made the highest grade in my class on state boards in communicable disease, a 99%," the former cadet recalled with pride.

Senior cadet nurses felt the anxiety and fear about what was to come after graduation, like taking state boards. Claris Gillund Syren said:

> Completing 3 years of study and hard work brought feelings of joy and exhilaration. But this happiness was mixed with the sadness of the impending separation from dear friends, the anxiety of making job decisions, and the apprehension of taking state boards.

The night before Zita Peterson Lindell, of Omaha Methodist Hospital School of Nursing in Nebraska, took the state board exams she and four cadet classmates stayed at her sister's apartment. "We hung the framed 'Nurses Prayer' on the wall and together repeated it before retiring. During our prayers the [framed copy] fell off the wall [and] onto the floor. We worried the incident might have been a bad omen."

At last, the graduation ceremony arrived, the most important ritual and reward of all. Cadets whose student hospital uniforms were blue and white striped, or other colors such as pink, green, or brown had the thrill of wearing white. Other special graduation designations included the addition of a special graduate cap or stripes, and a school pin—one that was unique to the school of nursing providing the diploma. For most, graduation was a rite of passage that evoked feelings of accomplishment and joy.

"I proudly wore my white uniform for the first time," said Donna Hardenburger Kennedy, "on the last day of my

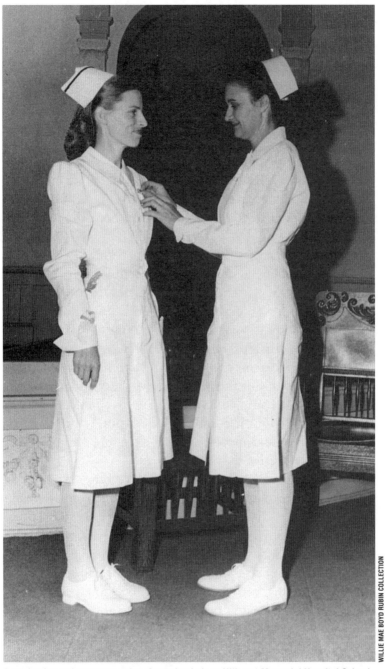

A graduating cadet nurse receives her school pin at Hillcrest Memorial Hospital School of Nursing at a special ceremony in Waco, Texas.

nursing school days at Lincoln General Hospital." Excited and head high, she arrived on the unit and received her assignment: "Special" a patient in isolation, which meant to care for one patient exclusively for the whole shift. "I spent the entire 8 hours wearing a gown, cap, and mask—feeling crushed because no one could tell that I was wearing a white uniform."

The first day after Darlene Pfaff Hornbacher graduated from the Trinity Hospital School of Nursing in Minot, North Dakota, she wore her long-sleeved, white uniform, a lovely handkerchief with tatted edging stuck in the upper left pocket, like a flower, with her school pin in the middle. Oh, what a day! "My little sister in training gave me a corsage to wear," Darlene said. "One of the doctors asked me if I had gotten married."

"We always wore white at Los Angeles County General Hospital and were used to it," said Dorothie Melvin Crowley, "but it was a thrill to remove the student shoulder patch and receive the school pin when we graduated." Wearing the school pin and having the black velvet stripe across their caps were the visible rewards for 3 years of study and work. "The freedom that came with the white uniform and the school pin," said Claribel Carlson Crews of Lincoln General Hospital, "outweighed the responsibilities that went with it."

At graduation, cadets felt much like they did as pre-cadets—eager to get on with their lives, but sad at leaving a special time behind. The big difference between capping and graduation? After graduation, members of the U.S. Cadet Nurse Corps went forth from their selected nursing programs prepared, confident, grateful, and ready to provide nursing knowledge and skills to the people of a nation who had made possible an education that would last a lifetime.

References

Petry, L. (1944a, September 5). The senior cadet period and some of its implications. (USPHS Memorandum No. 4). (RG90). Washington, DC: National Archives and Records Administration.

Petry, L. (1944b). Planning the senior cadet period. **American Journal of Nursing, 44**(1), 57-59.

U.S. Federal Security Agency. (1950). **U.S. cadet nurse corps 1943-1948.** (PHS Publication No. 38, p. 85). Washington, DC: United States Government Printing Office.

USPHS. (Circa 1944). **U.S. marine hospitals of the USPHS need senior cadets.** (N. E. Leaflet No. 2). Washington, DC: National Archives and Records Administration.

17

The Challenge to Tradition
by Paulie M. Perry

The U.S. Cadet Nurse Corps brought about many positive achievements that justified the Corps' existence, according to Phillip A. Kalisch, foremost historian researcher of the Corps. He said:

> What would have happened without this national effort to bolster nursing? Given the poor conditions of nursing education in the 1930s and the unprecedented demands of World War II, it is likely that too few nurses would have been available to furnish a safe, adequate, and humane level of health care. Such a situation would have impaired national security and severely undermined the nation's health care delivery system (Kalisch, 1988, p. 317).

The promotional campaign of the Corps not only successfully added to the number of student nurses, but also helped to elevate the status of women who joined the nursing profession. Ruth Stewart Powell attested to this change in the traditional prewar public opinion of nurses.

Ruth grew up in Nebraska during the Great Depression when the drought forced her family off the farm. "I attended 13 different schools because of family moves but was consistently the champion speller of my school. However I cried each time I had to say good-bye with the challenge of meeting new friends," said Ruth.

> I worked for my board and room while attending four different high schools and saved $5 each week for tuition for college. After

spending a semester at the Teachers College of the University of Nebraska, I realized I had a stronger desire to be a nurse then a teacher.

When I told my father of my ambition to become a nurse, he responded, "That kind of woman? Why?" Nevertheless he sold a cow so that my mother would have money to buy and sew the material for my student nurse uniform-blue and white striped fabric for the dress and plain white fabric for the aprons. The school of nursing I selected allowed incoming students to make their own uniforms, which reduced the tuition expense.

In February 1944 Ruth transferred to Lincoln General Hospital School of Nursing. "That brought a great day when I joined the Cadet Nurse Corps. I felt relieved to have my schooling paid for and have spending money besides," said Ruth.

While I was working in the surgical unit, my mother suddenly became ill and was admitted to Lincoln General with severe abdominal pains. Following gall-bladder surgery I waited in the recovery room ready to care for my mother.

When the surgical team wheeled mother into her room my father could only stare with fright in his eyes at the intravenous tubes running into his wife and the gallbladder and catheter drainage tubes running out of her. When he realized I could give Mother the care she needed he walked over to me in my white apron and striped uniform and put his arms around me. His eyes beamed through tears as he said, "We need this kind of woman in our family."

As change occurred across the nation, attitudes and the traditions in schools of nursing also changed. In Lincoln, Nebraska, the three schools of nursing, united by the mass induction of cadet nurses in the city's ceremony on May 13, 1944, began to develop other examples of camaraderie. The cadets from Lincoln General Hospital, Bryan Memorial Hospital, and St. Elizabeth Hospital schools of nursing played competitive games of softball in Lincoln. The schools formed Lincoln Student Nurses' League and rotated meetings among the three schools. Cadets made new friends and compared policies of their schools.

As a senior cadet at Lincoln General Hospital, I served on a committee with cadets from the other two schools of nursing to draft bylaws forming the Nebraska State Student Nurse Association. This organization became a reality a few years later.

The student body of Lincoln General Hospital instigated another change. As pre-cadets we had observed the discontent of upper classmates and the growing desire in other schools of nursing for student representation with the school administrators. Feelings of unrest became more intense until, as senior cadets, we had the desire, confidence, and support to make a difference in our status. The development of our strength of character, purpose, and resolve born during our cadet years was exemplified in the class motto we chose: Serve, Strive, Succeed!

Cadets took action for the formation of a student council by consulting members of the Lincoln General Hospital Board, instructors in the school of nursing, some alumnae, and interested citizens not in the nursing profession. Senior cadet Phyllis Wright Cerney spearheaded the petition the cadets presented to the director of nurses and the hospital administrator. The petition, in part, read:

> We ask the right to establish and maintain an effective Student Council ... to discuss problems freely and to air grievances, for the right to take part in formulating, maintaining, and enforcing rules and policies, and for the right to be heard before more than one person.

Although the last cadet nurse class at Lincoln General Hospital initiated the concept of a student government, 4 years passed before a student council became a reality at that school of nursing (Lincoln General Hospital School of Nursing Alumni Association, 1976).

Cadets brought about other improvements in their personal status. Students at the Protestant Deaconess Hospital School of Nursing in Evansville, Indiana, rebelled at the long-established tradition that required students to wear black stockings and black, laced shoes. Virginia Wakefield Broom recalled the following:

> Our class took our case to the director of nursing and the administrator and asked that we be allowed to wear white shoes and stockings after the capping ceremony. We argued that not only did the black stockings demean the students, but the cadets also suffered from increased foot infections.
>
> The administration listened to our pleas and changed the tradition. Our class blazed the trail and celebrated being the first class to wear "whites."

Cadet nurses provided 80% of the nursing care in civilian hospitals during the Corps' 5 years of existence. Cadets worked shifts in the hospital, attended classes, and were expected to study in the intervening hours. Miriam Morgan Bartlett remembered, "I had many colds, flu, 'mono' [infectious mononucleosis], and German measles while a cadet nurse [at] the University of Minnesota School of Nursing. We also experienced constant fatigue from our rigorous schedule of classes and hospital duty."

The administrative policies allowed 2 weeks sick leave, but Miriam had used all her leave and had an additional month to make up after her graduation in June 1945. "The school of nursing changed its long-established work schedule and decreased the work load for the next class," she said. Cadets welcomed this change in the traditional course of study.

The U.S. Cadet Nurse Corps, concerned for the health of its cadet nurses, required participating schools of nursing to provide adequate health services for students that included chest x-rays and TB testing. In its first year of existence, Corps' leaders feared the heavy work and study schedules, brought about by wartime demands on student nurses, might be detrimental to the health of young cadets (U.S. Federal Security Agency, 1950).

Before the '40s, each school of nursing set its own health standards and a wide range of diversity prevailed in student health programs. The Corps established minimum health requirements for schools participating in the Corps program.

In 1944 the USPHS launched the first comprehensive study of health programs for students in schools of nursing. The survey showed that 89% of the schools had a 48-hour workweek. More than half had no allowance for sick leave, and time missed for health reasons had to be made up. Most schools paid for hospitalization, x-rays, and laboratory tests. More than 200 schools of nursing had no prerequisite physical examination, nor did they require immunizations

COURTESY SIGNE S. COOPER

Cadet nurses at Milwaukee County Hospital display their summer uniforms. This hospital was one of 24 institutions that participated in the U.S. Cadet Nurse Corps in Wisconsin.

for diphtheria, smallpox, and typhoid fever (Davis, Felix, Silverman, & Altenderfer, 1945).

In October 1944 the Surgeon General appointed a committee to study nursing school health practices. The program formulated by this committee was adopted in May 1945. This action set a precedent for standardizing health programs for students enrolled in schools of nursing, a significant outcome of the Corps (Davis et al., 1945).

Nurse education consultants of the Corps used this information in their consultative service to schools of nursing. Under the guidance of the USPHS, many of the schools reported improvement in their students' health. An unexpected but extremely valuable by-product of the nurse education consultant visits to the schools participating in the Corps program was the "1125 School Study" (Kalisch & Kalisch, 1975).

Eighty-seven percent, or 1,125 of the 1,295 nursing schools were in the U.S. Cadet Nurse Corps and were a part of this federally sponsored survey. This figure surpassed two previous national surveys that relied totally on paper reports for their data, with 74% and 81% of the schools represented (Kalisch & Kalisch, 1975).

The success of the 1125 study was largely because of visits made by nurse education consultants, an unprecedented experience for most schools of nursing. The investigators for the study compiled a wealth of information, which became a prime reference for nursing educators (Kalisch & Kalisch, 1975).

The results gave added impetus to a movement toward accreditation of schools of nursing by a national professional body. "Our consultants aided many schools of nursing in the advancement of their curriculum," said Corps Director Lucile Petry. "They served as liaison between schools of nursing and community educational institutions."

Corps Director Lucile Petry told of a consultant who made a visit to a school of nursing where the director of education deplored her lack of competent instructors. "I do not know what we are going to do," the director said.

Down the road from that hospital, a community college suffered from insufficient students because of many young people serving in the armed forces or working in defense industries. The consultant encouraged the two institutions to work together with the result that the community college provided the science courses for the school of nursing.

Instead of competing for students, hospital schools of nursing and small colleges across the nation found that each had a role in educating nurses. The colleges were equipped to teach science courses and the diploma hospital programs were prepared to teach clinical nursing courses. "By working together they set a precedent for the future of nursing education," said Corps Director Lucile Petry (L. Petry, personal communication, March 1998).

Social mores also changed. In the '30s most businesses and school boards did not hire married women. When America found itself engaged in war with a desperate labor shortage, women were needed and "courted" to work in factories, join the military, and return to civilian nursing. Married, inactive nurses were urged to fill the growing need for health care providers.

An article in the April 1942 issue of the *American Journal of Nursing* stated:

> Our married nurses, we believe, will gladly nurse for victory when they realize that the opportunities of those responsible for the care in civilian hospitals should be heeded because the care of these patients is such an extremely important part of the gigantic task of winning the war ("Nursing for Victory," 1942, pp. 400-401).

But what about married status for student nurses? It had long been the tradition that schools of nursing would not admit married women and would dismiss those students who married before graduation. With only a few exceptions, most nursing schools in the '40s did not accept married women.

The Corps did not bar married women from its ranks but allowed officials at each school of nursing to make their own rules. Did love and marriage affect cadets' careers? The following responses by former cadets provide answers to this question:

> Because of the war going on, the men were either too young or too old. We cadets had few dates (Thelma Barstad Bushnell, Bismarck Hospital School of Nursing, North Dakota).

> I didn't have a problem because my fiancé was in the Army the same time I was in nurses' training (Virginia Marks Prehn, Butterworth Hospital of Grand Rapids, Michigan).

> Love and marriage had to wait until I graduated. My boyfriend didn't want to wait, so he married someone else (Alice Jans Donley, Sioux Falls Valley Hospital School of Nursing in Sioux Falls, South Dakota).

> I was one of the first students allowed to be married while in training. I had to be a senior cadet and have written permission from both sets of parents and my fiancé's commanding officer (Lucille North Vogt, Los Angeles County General Hospital School of Nursing).

> There was no conflict between Madison General Hospital School of Nursing and love and marriage because marriage was not permitted and love was squelched as much as possible (Barbara Oetzel Lenthart, Madison General Hospital School of Nursing, Wisconsin).

The University of Nebraska Medical Center College of Nursing in Omaha broke tradition and gave permission for the marriage of 10 junior cadets, including Ruth Ann Schultze Vogel. When Ruth Ann's fiancé came home on furlough, they had a Sunday afternoon church wedding in Stanton, Nebraska, with a reception at the Schultze farm. "We stayed at a hotel in Omaha on our wedding night but the next morning I attended class at the hospital," she said. They spent a few days together before her new husband left for the European Theater of Operations. For 18 months they communicated by censored mail, which came sporadically.

Teatime at Portsmouth Naval Hospital in Virginia gave cadet nurses an opportunity to discuss the military aspects of their time spent at the base. Lt. Cmdr. Leola Scheips (LeBar), seated in center, organized the social program for cadets spending their last 6 months at the base.

Shirley Morrison Francisco remembered the following:

In 1948, when I was a senior cadet at the Meadville City Hospital School of Nursing in Pennsylvania, a classmate secretly married her fiancé who had just returned from the military. This was forbidden and she hesitated before confiding in her fellow cadets because she felt embarrassed, as well as devastated, knowing she would have to leave school. So two other students and I decided something had to be done.

After working all night we met outside the superintendent's office. We sat there until he appeared at 9:00 a.m. and ambushed him as he unlocked his door. We spent the next hour explaining why the antiquated rule of forbidding married women to be student nurses needed to be changed. Probably to get rid of us he finally agreed to present the situation to the board of directors. We marched off to the dorm to sleep hoping our strategy would be successful.

The superintendent was as good as his word. He did get the rule changed. Discrimination against women who married had ended at our nursing school at last.

Summary

The federal government's establishment of the U.S. Cadet Nurse Corps (the largest federal nursing program) to remedy the shortage of nurses precipitated by World War II accomplished its mission with the graduation of 124,065 nurses during its years of existence, 1943 to 1948 (Willever, 1994). Furthermore, the business relationship between the Corps and the schools of nursing across the nation was a unique experiment and a break from traditional methods of funding. The federal government, through the USPHS, allocated large sums of taxpayer money for nursing education that helped pave the way for future federal grants to educational institutions. And all of this effort ultimately helped increase and improve the health status of the entire nation (Willever, 1994).

Other positive outcomes came about as a result of the Corps. For example, the Corps' program challenged tradition by allowing 17- and 18-year-old women to serve their country in uniform and not be discriminated against because of race, creed, or color. The Corps was also responsible for accelerating the instruction in nursing education so that students finished courses in 30 instead of 36 months. And senior cadets were able to broaden their nursing experience by having the opportunity to choose nursing services outside their "home" schools.

Personal and social outcomes changed as a result of cadets' experiences. Cadets surreptitiously broke the bonds of tradition by challenging archaic rules. Cadet nurses envisioned a better tomorrow by challenging their individual schools of nursing to change the student uniform, permit marriage, and establish student councils. These changes ultimately led to an adjustment of social standards for student nurses. Nurses gained power and prestige when they took the initiative and worked against outdated prejudices and practices.

In earlier years Isabelle Maitland Stewart warned that the desire of student nurses to give service and alleviate human suffering was often thwarted by excessive discipline (Stewart, 1940). Cadet nurses all too frequently found this to be true. Through teamwork with the USPHS and the institutions in which they trained, the U.S. Cadet Nurse Corps heeded Stewart's urging to create a more democratic environment for students and nurses.

From the USPHS offices in Washington, D.C., to the dorm rooms in Lincoln, Nebraska, and other schools of nursing throughout the nation, Corps members challenged tradition, improving nursing education for generations to follow. What a paradox! Dr. Bonnie Bullough (1976) a valued historian said, "The Cadet Nurse Corps, which used students as workers, set precedents for federal aid to nursing education which later helped schools of nursing escape from the apprenticeship system."

The national promotion of the U.S. Cadet Nurse Corps was initiated with fervor and met with phenomenal support and success. Corps Director Lucile Petry (Leone) concluded, "Without the tumult of World War II, we might have waited more decades to open our eyes to the bigness of nursing (Willever, 1994).

References

Bullough, B. (1976). Nurses in American history. The lasting impact of World War II on nursing. **American Journal of Nursing, 76(1),** 118-120.

Davis, B.M., Felix, R.H., Silverman, C., & Altenderfer, M.E. (1945). **A study of nursing school health practices and a recommended health program for student nurses.** (PHS Supplement, No. 189, pp. 1-6). (RG90). Washington, DC: National Archives and Records Administration.

Kalisch, P. (1988). Why not launch a new cadet nurse corps? **American Journal of Nursing, 88(3),** 317.

Kalisch, B.J., & Kalisch, P.A. (1975). Slaves, servants, or saints? An analysis of the system of nurse training in the United States 1873-1948. **Nursing Forum, 14(3),** 253-254.

Lincoln General Hospital School of Nursing Alumni Association. (1976). **Lincoln General Hospital School of Nursing History: September 7, 1925 - May 14, 1976.** Lincoln, NE: Author.

Nursing for victory. (1942). **American Journal of Nursing, 42(4),** 400-401.

Stewart, I.M. (1940). Nursing education and national defense. **American Journal of Nursing, 40(12),** 1382.

U.S. Federal Security Agency. (1950). **U.S. cadet nurse corps 1943-1948.** (PHS publication No. 38, pp. 54-56). Washington DC: United States Government Printing Office.

Willever, H. (1994). **50th anniversary cadet nurse corp** (pp. 1, 14, 15). Washington, DC: American Nurses Association Foundation.

EPILOGUE

by Thelma M. Robinson

The Cadet Nurse Project initiated in 1993 by my sister, Paulie Morey Perry, and myself began with the search for journal, magazine, and newspaper articles about the U.S. Cadet Nurse Corps. Days were spent in the National Archives Record Administration in Washington, D.C., and the National Library of Medicine in Bethesda, Md., searching for orginial documents. Our project was first introduced to the public in *The American Nurse* (Robinson, 1994). In May 1994 at the 50th year Cadet Nurse Corps Commemorative Conference in Bethesda, Md., Paulie and I presented a poster session and distributed our brochure informing former cadet nurses about our project and inviting them to participate (Perry & Robinson, 1994).

Recruitment efforts were continued by contacting schools of nursing and alumni associations. Our invitation was extended to anyone who had been associated with the Corps such as former instructors and directors in nursing. The response we received was enthusiastic. These women wanted the cadet nurse story told and supported our project by sharing stories, photographs, memorabilia and sending unsolicited funds. More than 380 women representing 33 states plus the District of Columbia and 121 schools of nursing joined in this nationwide project (Robinson, 2000).

The U.S. Cadet Nurse Corps offered those who joined a free education that lasted a lifetime. Participants in the *Cadet Nurse Project* were asked if this promise had been fulfilled. Overwhelmingly the answer from the former cadets, who were also the children of the Great Depression years, was Yes!

More than 75% of the participants in this nationwide project reported that without the Corps they would not have had a career in nursing. These women continued to serve their communities as nurses for an average of 28 years (Robinson, 1999).

Some used their experience as a springboard to another profession to serve others.

Sharon Tanagi Aburano was one who practiced nursing for only 7 years. Although she didn't spend a lifetime in nursing, the discipline and academic stimulus acquired as a cadet nurse helped her set high goals. She obtained three academic degrees that enabled her to put into practice the slogan of St. Mary's Hospital School of Nursing in Rochester, Minnesota: "Enter in to learn, Go forth to serve."

Sharon continued to serve throughout her life as a school librarian. She was nominated twice for the outstanding "Excellence in Education" award in the Seattle School District.

She was also one of the 110,000 Japanese Americans who were transported to one of 10 relocation camps throughout the seven states. The Corps gave several hundred young women like Sharon an opportunity to show their devotion to America and provided them a tuition-free education. All seven Japanese American women participating in this project shared their appreciation and indebtedness to the Corps.

The Corps gave retired Colonel Melina Marzocchi LeDuc the beginning of a lifetime education in nursing. Melina grew up in a traditional Italian family. She desperately wanted to be a nurse, but in her family only the boys were provided with an education. She was just a girl. "I do not know what would have happened to my life had the Cadet Nurse Corps not been available," she said.

At the age of 17 Melina entered Barre City Hospital School of Nursing in Vermont, joined the Corps and soon

Retired Col. Melina Marzocchi LeDuc, former cadet nurse who served in the Gulf War, said, "I wanted to show that we cadets were still active and viable, willing and eager to serve our country."

after graduation she began serving in veterans' hospitals. She had always wanted to be in the military, so in 1967 she joined the Army Reserves, working on the weekends for the Army and during the week for the VA. "I had the best of both worlds," she said.

Along the way Melina obtained both a bachelor's and a master's degree and served as a VA nurse for 37 years. In August 1990 she received a call from the Pentagon asking if she would be interested in becoming active at Fort Benning as Chief Nurse of Surgery and Emergency Medical Services. She accepted with the stipulation that if her Army Reserve Medical Detachment was called for active duty she would be allowed to go with them. In December of that year, her unit was deployed to Saudi Arabia.

In Saudi Arabia, Melina, then 63 years old, worked 12-hour shifts, 7 days a week in the operating room. She cared for Iraqi prisoners of war in addition to Americans. She experienced nightly air raid alerts and had to interrupt preparations for surgery in order to put on a mask and protective gear. She cared for injured military personnel when a SKUD missile hit the American barracks in Dhahran located near Melina's tent. Later she said proudly, "I wanted to show that we cadets were still active and viable, willing and eager to serve our country."

Sarah Gomez Erlach's financial challenge was solved when she joined the Corps. When she graduated in 1945, she entered the U.S. Army Nurse Corps beginning an association with the Army that spanned 34 years and ended with her retirement as a full colonel. In 1949 Sarah obtained a bachelor of science degree. A year later she met and married Gregory Erlach. Her husband, who had served in World War II, re-enlisted to serve in the Korean War. He was killed 6 months later, then Sarah lost the baby she was carrying. Devastated with her losses, Sarah threw herself into work, trying to improve the health care delivery system to the poor. Later with sponsorship of her superiors at Alameda County, California, she enrolled in the master's degree program in public health at the University of Minnesota (Grant, 1995).

With an MPH degree, Sarah began working to improve health care for migrant populations. Years later, in 1995, she was awarded the University of California, San Francisco, highest medal because of her positive effect on health in that state. According to Dean Jane Norbeck of the school of nursing at the University of California, San Francisco, "Sarah was doing bilingual, bicultural, interdisciplinary health care long before these terms were widely used.... She's a very determined person" (Grant, 1995).

On January 19, 1997, a small group of friends and former cadets gathered to help Lucile Petry Leone, emeritus director of the Cadet Nurse Corps celebrate her 95th birthday. While sharing memories "Miss Petry" recalled that a draft specifically for nurses was debated as World War II dragged on. She told about her office putting out a call to recently graduated cadets reporting the desperate need for nurses. They joined the military in record numbers and the crisis was abated. Thanks to the cadets and other events the end of the war moved closer. She said, "Cadets always came through."

Credit for the success of the U.S. Cadet Nurse Corps goes to Lucile Petry Leone for her ability to lead. Rear Admiral Carolyn Beth Mazzella, chief nurse officer and member of the USPHS Professional Advisory Committee for nursing sent congratulations and a letter that read:

> Your leadership of the Cadet Nurse Corps opened new horizons in nursing as a profession, in nursing education, and in service. Your insistence on equality and quality in schools of nursing pioneered integration. And your rise to assistant surgeon general created career paths for women in the uniformed services and for the women who followed. We salute you and thank you for your vision and excellence in nursing.

In compiling the cadet nurse stories over the past 7 years, Paulie, my sister and coauthor, and I engaged in weekly telephone talks. Sometimes it was difficult to keep on target. Mark, Paulie's talented son-in-law, who helped us design "The Cadet Nurse Corps-A Story Unfolding" brochure, was dying of cancer. When Paulie hung up the telephone after our conversations, she took her laptop computer and headed for the hospice just as she did every day. "I am giving Mark old-fashioned nursing care," Paulie said one day when we talked.

Chemotherapy, radiation, laser-knife, and alternative medicine had failed. Now caring and a gentle touch were all the help that could be offered. Technology comes and goes, but these two nursing ingredients will always be needed.

Dorothy Klingla Freeze, cadet nurse from Los Angeles County General Hospital School of Nursing, said it well when she said:

It has been a wonderful time, with so many changes not only in nursing, but in society as a whole. I am happy to have been a part of it. My greatest reward was to see the pride in my parents' eyes when I completed my nursing education. My father became my strongest booster and always introduced me as cadet nurse Dorothy.

Nursing gave me more than nursing skills. Through nursing I learned tolerance, patience, perseverance, and, I hope, compassion. Nursing encompassed my entire adult life. Nursing provided me much more than a living. Nursing gave me the self-discipline, self-reliance, and the self-confidence to weather the stormy times in life.

Cadet nurses leave as their legacy the hope that those who aspire to a career in nursing will not be denied the education needed to achieve that goal. Without the U.S. Cadet Nurse Corps many women would not have accomplished their dream of becoming a nurse. Fifty years have come and gone since cadet nurses wore the Maltese cross on their sleeves, but the spirit of caring lives forever in their hearts.

References

Grant, J. (1995, Summer). Fighting for migrant health: Profile of Sarah Gomez Erlach. Alumni News University of California, San Francisco, 13(1), 2-4.

Perry, P.M., & Robinson, T.M. (1994). Cadet nurse corps: A story unfolding. [Brochure]. Aurora, CO: Authors.

Robinson, T.M. (1994). Remembering the corps. The American Nurse, 26(3), 4.

Robinson, T.M. (1999, October). Cadet Nurse Corps: Winning the war on the home front. Poster Session presented at the annual conference of the American Association for the History of Nursing, Boston, MA.

Robinson, T.M. (2000, Summer). The cadet nurse project. American Association for the History of Nursing Bulletin, 67, 10.

Additional Resources

(used in preparation of this book)

American Association for the History of Nursing. (1999). **Nursing history review, Vol. 7.** Philadelphia, PA: University of Pennsylvania Press.

American Association for the History of Nursing. (1997). **Nursing history review, Vol. 5.** Philadelphia, PA: University of Pennsylvania Press.

American Association for the History of Nursing. (1995). **Nursing history review, Vol. 3.** Philadelphia, PA: University of Pennsylvania Press

Anderson, K. (1981). **Wartime women: Sex roles, family relations and the status of women during World War II.** Westport, CT: Greenwood Press.

Bailey, B., & Farber, D. (1992). **The first strange place: Race and sex in World War II Hawaii.** Baltimore, MD: Johns Hopkins University Press.

Baxandell, R., Gordon, L., & Reverby, S. (1976). **America's working women.** New York: Vantage Books-Division of Random House.

Brown, E.L. (1948). **Nursing for the future. A report prepared for the National Nursing Council.** New York: Russell Sage Foundation.

Brueggemann, D.W. (1992). **The U.S. Cadet Nurse Corps 1943-1948: The Nebraska experience.** Unpublished master's thesis, University of Nebraska, Omaha.

Bullough, V.L., & Bullough, B. (1978). **The care of the sick: Emergence of modern nursing.** New York: Prodist.

Bullough, V.L., Church, O.M., & Stein, A.P. (Eds.). (1988). American nursing: A bibliographical dictionary. Volumes I and II. New York: Garland Reference Library of Social Science.

Bullough, V.L., & Sentz, L. (Eds.). (2000). **American nursing: A biographical dictionary.** Volume III. New York: Springer.

Butterworth Hospital School of Nursing. (1985). Ninety-five years of nursing education, 1890-1995. Grand Rapids, MI: Author.

Campbell, D.A. (1984). **Women at war with America: Private lives in a patriotic era.** Cambridge, MA: Harvard University Press.

Candy, B.H. (Ed.). (1984). **Remembering things past: A heritage of excellence.** Minneapolis, MN: University of Minnesota School of Nursing.

Carnegie, M.E. (1991). **The path we tread: Blacks in nursing 1854-1990** (2nd ed.). New York: National League for Nursing.

Chafe, W.H. (1972). **The American woman: Her changing social, economic, and political roles, 1920-1970.** New York: Oxford University Press.

Cleary, B.B. (1994). **Robert Packer school of nursing: A history 1901-1989.** Endwell, NY: Lewis Group.

Cooper, H.M., Munich, A.A., & Squier, S.M. (Eds.). (1989). Arms and the woman: War, gender, and literacy representation. Chapel Hill, NC: University of North Carolina Press.

Deloughery, G.L. (1977). **History and trends of professional nursing** (8th ed.). St. Louis, MO: Mosby.

Dietz, L.D., & Lehozky, A.R. (1967). **History and modern nursing.** Philadelphia: Davis.

Dock, L.L., & Stewart, I.M. (1938). **A short history of nursing.** New York: Putnam & Sons.

Dolan, J., Fitzpatrick, M.L., & Herrman, E.K. (1983). Nursing in society: A historical perspective (15th ed.). Philadelphia, PA: Saunders.

Donahue, M.P. (1996). **Nursing the finest art: An illustrated history** (2nd ed.). St. Louis, MO: Mosby.

Elders, G.H. (1974). **Children of the great depression: Social change in life experiences.** Chicago: The University of Chicago Press.

Gluck, S.B. (1978). **Rosie the riveter revisited: Women, the war and social change.** New York: New American Library.

Goostray, S. (1969). **Memories: Half a century of nursing.** (Nursing Archives, Division of Special Collection). Boston: University Libraries.

Gray, J. (1960). **Education for nursing: A history of the University of Minnesota School.** Minneapolis, MN: University of Minnesota Press.

Griffin, G.J., & Griffin, J.K. (1969). Jensen's history and trends of professional nursing. St. Louis, MO: Mosby.

Gruhzit-Hoyt, O. (1995). They also served America: Women in World War II. New York: Carol Publishing.

Hartman, S.M. (1982). The home front and beyond: American women in 1940s. Boston, MA: Twayne Publishers.

Heinemann, S. (1996). Timelines of American women's history. New York: Berkley Publishing.

Higonnet, M.R., Jensen, J. Michel, S. , & Weitz, M.C. (Eds.). (1987). Behind the lines: Gender and two world wars. New Haven, CT: Yale University Press.

Hine, D.C. (1989). Black women in white: Racial conflict and cooperation in the nursing profession. Bloomington, IN: Indiana University Press.

Holm, J.M. (1992). Women in the military: An Unfinished revolution. Nocato, CA: Presidio.

Holm, J.M., & Bellafaire, J. (Eds.). (1998). In defense of a nation: Service women of World War II. Washington, DC: Military Women's Press.

Honey, M. (1984). Creating Rosie the riveter: Class, gender, and propaganda during World War II. Amherst, MA: University of Massachusetts Press.

Irons, P. (1983). Justice at war: The inside story of Japanese-American internment. New York: Oxford University Press.

Kalisch, P.A., & Kalisch, B.J. (1980). The federal influence and impact on nursing. Ann Arbor, MI: University of Michigan.

Kalisch, P.A., & Kalisch, B.J. (1995). The advance of American nursing (3rd ed.). Philadelphia: Lippincott.

Kelly. L.Y. (1991). Dimensions of professional nursing (6th ed). New York: Pergamon Press.

Lagemann, E.C. (Ed.). (1983). Nursing history: New perspective, new possibilities. New York: Teachers College, Columbia University.

Litoff, J.B., & Smith, D.C. (1991). Since you went away to World War II: Letters from American women on the home front. New York: Oxford University Press.

Litoff, J.B., & Smith, D.C. (1994). We're in this war too: World War II letters from American women in uniform. New York: Oxford University Press.

Maddox, R.J. (1992). The United States and World War II. Boulder, CO: Westview Press.

Marks, G., & Beatty, W.K. (1976). Epidemics. New York: Scribner.

McBryde, B. (1985). Quiet heroines: Nurses of the second World War. London: Hogarth Press.

Melosh, B. (1982). The physician's hand: Work, culture and conflict in American nursing. Philadelphia: Temple University Press.

Reverby, S.M. (1987). Ordered to care: The dilemma of American nursing, 1850-1945. Cambridge, MA: University Press.

Roberts, M.N. (1961). American nursing history and interpretation. New York: Macmillan.

Rowland, H. (1984). The nurse's almanac. Rockville, MD: Aspen.

Schneider, D., & Schneider, C.F. (1993). Women in the workplace. Santa Barbara, CA: ABC-CLIO.

Schorr, T.M., & Zimmerman, A. (1988). Making choices, taking chances. St. Louis, MO: Mosby.

Shyrock, R.H. (1959). The history of nursing: An interpretation of the social and medical factors involved. Philadelphia, PA: Saunders.

Smute, R.W. (1971). Women and work in America. New York: Schocken Books.

Stewart, I.M., & Austin, A.L. (1962). A history of nursing (5th ed.). New York: Putnam and Sons.

Terkle, S. (1984). The good war: An oral history of World War II. New York: Pantheon Books.

United Sates Federal Security Agency, Public Health Service, Division of Nurse Education. (1943, August). Schools of nursing approved by respective state board of examiners. Washington, DC: Library of Congress.

Weatherford, D. (1990). American women and World War II. New York: Facts on File.

Appendix

Schools of Nursing with Cadet Nurse Alumni Participating in the Cadet Nurse Project.

Alabama
  Tuskegee Institute University

California
  Children's Hospital School of Nursing, San Francisco
  Los Angeles County General Hospital School of Nursing, Los Angeles
  St. Joseph Hospital School of Nursing, Orange County
  St. Luke's Hospital School of Nursing, San Francisco
  San Bernardino County Hospital School of Nursing, San Bernardino
  Stanford University School of Nursing, San Francisco
  University of California School of Nursing, San Francisco

Colorado
  Children's Hospital School of Nursing, Denver
  Colorado Training School for Nurses, Denver
  Presbyterian Hospital School of Nursing, Denver
  Seton Hospital School of Nursing, Colorado Springs
  University of Colorado School of Nursing, Denver

Connecticut
  Bridgeport Hospital School of Nursing, Bridgeport
  Yale University School of Nursing, New Haven

Delaware
  Memorial Hospital School of Nursing, Wilmington

District of Columbia
  Garfield Memorial Hospital School of Nursing, Washington, DC

Georgia
  Emory University School of Nursing, Atlanta

Iowa
  Jennie Edmundson Hospital School of Nursing, Council Bluffs
  Lutheran Hospital School of Nursing, Sioux City

Illinois
  Michael Reese Hospital School of Nursing, Chicago
  Swedish Covenant Hospital School of Nursing, Chicago

Indiana
  Indianapolis General Hospital School of Nursing, Indianapolis
  Protestant Deaconess Hospital School of Nursing, Evansville
  Wishard Memorial Hospital School of Nursing, Indianapolis

Kentucky
  Kentucky Baptist Hospital School of Nursing, Louisville

Louisiana
  Baptist Hospital School of Nursing, Alexandria
  Hotel Dieu Hospital School of Nursing, New Orleans

Maine
  Eastern Maine General Hospital School of Nursing, Bangor
  Mercy Hospital School of Nursing, Portland

Massachusetts
  Beth Israel Hospital School of Nursing, Boston
  Massachusetts General Hospital School of Nursing, Boston
  Peter Bent Brigham Hospital School of Nursing, Boston
  Quincy City Hospital School of Nursing, Quincy
  Salem Hospital School of Nursing, Salem

Maryland
  Johns Hopkins Hospital School of Nursing, Baltimore

Michigan
  Blodgett Memorial Hospital School of Nursing, Grand Rapids
  Butterworth Hospital School of Nursing, Grand Rapids
  Henry Ford Hospital School of Nursing, Detroit
  Highland Park General Hospital School of Nursing, Highland Park
  St. Camillius Borgess Hospital School of Nursing, Kalamazoo

Minnesota
  Abbott Hospital School of Nursing, Minneapolis
  College of St. Catherine School of Nursing, St. Paul
  Eitel Hospital School of Nursing, Minneapolis
  Kahler Hospital School of Nursing, Rochester
  Northwestern Hospital School of Nursing, Minneapolis
  St. Luke's Hospital School of Nursing, Duluth
  St. Mary's Hospital School of Nursing, Rochester
  Swedish Hospital School of Nursing, Minneapolis
  University of Minnesota School of Nursing, Minneapolis

Missouri
  St. Louis City Hospital School of Nursing, St. Louis
  St. Louis Jewish Hospital School of Nursing, St. Louis
  St. Luke's Hospital School of Nursing, Kansas City
  University of Missouri School of Nursing, Columbia

Montana
  Montana State University School of Nursing, Great Falls

Nebraska
  Bryan Memorial Hospital School of Nursing, Lincoln
  Lincoln General Hospital School of Nursing, Lincoln
  Mary Lanning Memorial Hospital School of Nursing, Hastings
  Nebraska Methodist Hospital School of Nursing, Omaha
  St. Elizabeth Hospital School of Nursing, Lincoln
  St. Francis Hospital School of Nursing, Grand Island
  St. Joseph Hospital School of Nursing, Omaha
  University of Nebraska School of Nursing, Omaha

New Jersey
   Englewood Hospital School of Nursing, Englewood
   West Jersey Hospital School of Nursing, Camden

New York
   Arnot-Ogden Memorial Hospital School of Nursing, Elmira
   Bellevue Hospital School of Nursing, New York
   Ellis Hospital School of Nursing, Schenectady
   Flower-Fifth Avenue Hospital School of Nursing, New York
   Genesee Hospital School of Nursing, Rochester
   Highland Hospital School of Nursing, Rochester
   Keuka College School of Nursing, Keuka Park
   Mercy Hospital School of Nursing, Buffalo
   Our Lady of Victory School of Nursing, Kingston
   Rochester General Hospital School of Nursing, Rochester
   Rochester State Hospital, Rochester
   St. Luke's Hospital School of Nursing, New York
   St. Mary' Hospital School of Nursing, Rochester
   Sisters of Charity Hospital School of Nursing, Buffalo
   State University of Plattsburg School of Nursing, Plattsburg
   University of Rochester School of Nursing, Rochester

North Carolina
   Duke University School of Nursing, Durham

North Dakota
   Bismarck Evangelical Hospital School of Nursing, Bismarck
   Good Samaritan Hospital School of Nursing, Rugby
   St. Alexius Hospital School of Nursing, Bismarck
   Trinity Hospital School of Nursing, Minot

Ohio
   Akron City Hospital School of Nursing, Akron
   Frances Payne Bolton Hospital School of Nursing, Cleveland
   Mercy Hospital School of Nursing, Hamilton
   Miami Valley Hospital School of Nursing, Dayton
   Middleton Hospital School of Nursing, Middleton
   University of Cincinnati School of Nursing, Cincinnati
   Youngstown Hospital School of Nursing, Youngstown

Pennsylvania
   Altoona General Hospital School of Nursing, Altoona
   Conemaugh Valley Hospital School of Nursing, Johnstown
   Hospital of the Protestant Episcopal Church School of Nursing, Philadelphia
   Harrisburg Hospital School of Nursing, Harrisburg
   Meadville Hospital School of Nursing, Meadville
   Methodist Hospital School of Nursing, Philadelphia
   Robert Packer Hospital School of Nursing, Sayre

South Dakota
   Presentation Hospital School of Nursing, Aberdeen
   Sioux Falls Valley Hospital School of Nursing, Sioux Falls

Tennessee
   Baroness Erlanger School of Nursing, Chattanooga
   Vanderbilt University School of Nursing, Nashville

Texas
Hillcrest Memorial Hospital School of Nursing, Waco
Lubbock Memorial Hospital School of Nursing, Lubbock
St. Paul Hospital School of Nursing, Dallas
West Texas Hospital School of Nursing, Lubbock

Vermont
Vermont Barre City Hospital School of Nursing, Barre City

Virginia
Hampton Training School for Nurses, Hampton
Roanoke Memorial Hospital School of Nursing, Roanoke
St. Philip Hospital School of Nursing, Richmond

Washington
King County Harborview School of Nursing, Seattle
Tacoma General Hospital School of Nursing, Tacoma
University of Washington School of Nursing, Seattle

Wisconsin
Columbia Hospital School of Nursing, Milwaukee
Madison General Hospital School of Nursing, Madison
Milwaukee County Hospital School of Nursing, Milwaukee

West Virginia
Ohio Valley General Hospital School of Nursing, Wheeling
St. Mary's Hospital School of Nursing, Huntington